THE LITTLE BOOK
OF EVERYDAY SOUL

LILLIE GOODRICH

The
LITTLE BOOK
of EVERYDAY
SOUL

Prima Publishing

Published by Prima Publishing, Roseville, California. Member of the Crown Publishing Group, a division of Random House, Inc., New York.

PRIMA PUBLISHING and colophon are trademarks of Random House, Inc., registered with the United States Patent and Trademark Office.

Library of Congress Cataloging-in-Publication Data
Goodrich, Lillie.
   The little book of everyday soul / Lillie Goodrich
      p.   cm.
   ISBN 0-7615-6364-4
   1. Conduct of life. I. Title.
   BJ1581.2 .G66   2002
   170'.44—dc21   2002028535

02 03 04 05 06 HH 10 9 8 7 6 5 4 3 2 1
Printed in the United States of America

First Edition

Visit us online at www.primapublishing.com

This Little Book is dedicated to John, my soul partner, who gives me the profound experience of unconditional love. His true love grounds me in my heart, here on Earth, which allows me to intuitively channel the gifts I now share with people and animals. I am forever grateful for his gifts to me along with the life we've built surrounded by our dogs and cats on our farm, Glen Highland.

As we live in this commitment to God, then shall all the Angels in the universe rejoice in the dance of life which we shall always do together.

I love you, John

CONTENTS

ACKNOWLEDGMENTS

A special thanks to the important people who assisted me in sharing this book:

Mary Swanson, who provided profound guidance at the most important times in my life; Deborah Kremins, who assisted me through transition after transition; Gina Garrubbo, who offered deep friendship through the twists and turns of life; Alison Freeland, who held the energy of God when I was searching for answers; Alice Feinstein, who felt the truth of what this book could be for others and made it a reality; Libby Larson, who understood the words of this book and improved it; and, most importantly, John Andersen, who birthed Glen Highland Farm with me and joins in the soulful life we now live.

And a very important thank you to all the animals who jumped into my heart, thankfully opened it more fully, and shared the truths that matter: Fritz, Barney, Remy, Luke, Katie, Major, Magic, Darcy, Haley, Fly, Gibson, Witt, Ema, Flynn, Tigger, Sable, Sasha, Goldie, Moxie, and Nickie. Their generous, unconditional love shaped who I am today.

OPENING THE DOOR

Changing the way you see life is a day-by-day experience. Being able to focus on principles that are important as you go through day-to-day living is like having a lifeline out at sea in a raging storm. Just when a big wave is about to drag you under, an important principle can pull you out to see clearly again.

That's the purpose of *The Little Book of Everyday Soul*.

Numerous books offer answers to nourishing your soul and provide in-depth understanding of spirituality, but not much is available that serves, day by day, as a reminder of the key principles of soulful living. This is not an affirmation book or meditation book; this is a little book full of big information, presented simply so everyone can connect with and know what matters.

If you choose to read and use this book, you'll get the greatest benefit if you focus and consciously digest what is written. I suggest that you do not read this book cover to cover. It's meant as a guide to living with your Soul—ten chapters, each one giving you a new way to understand and re-create your life. Each chapter provides a clear focus for shifting perspective, changing beliefs, and, ultimately, changing your life. Together, the concepts create a spiritual handbook with simple direction. It's a practical way to tap into spiritual principles as a part of daily living.

Here are two ways to proceed:

Consider committing to a ten-week program, reading a chapter each week, then putting it into practice. Do not move on to the next chapter until you've understood the principles of the current chapter and have applied them to your life. In this way, *The Little Book of Everyday Soul* is a course that helps you strengthen your inner wisdom.

Or try opening the book to a chapter that "calls" to you. Digest what you read and know that whatever you have found is exactly what you need at that moment. Like a spiritual handbook, *The Little Book of Everyday Soul* is there whenever you need perspective.

However you choose to experience what you're about to read, please understand that the depth of what is here is a lifetime's work. My commitment to my own personal growth over the last sixteen years led me to this information. I wish I could have found it in one book, a work that I could have used over and over and over again as guidance. It didn't yet exist. I hope what I have written here is helpful to you in your journey.

In considering the messages of *The Little Book of Everyday Soul,* understand that this was a private journey until two years ago when this book was born. Two events linked together, prompting me to write.

Late one weekend, I watched my beloved partner lying in agony with a sickness that could kill him. I had waited years to find this man and then helplessly watched in uncertainty, wondering if he was about to be taken. Nothing in my repertoire of healing could help. His illness was not mine to handle. The deepest pain plagued my heart; I was shaken to the core about what this loss would mean for me. I held back my rage at the destiny that stared me in the face and, instead, prayed with intensity for guidance.

At the same time, my sweet, adorable cat, Remy, became ill with cancer. She had been my companion, my entrusted partner in life, helping me with my heart's longing. When no one was there, Remy was. And her continual request for love finally awoke in me the realization that she was teaching me how to love another. No one else had demanded that I stay in my heart, paying attention to love. Everyone else had let me run away and hide. But now she, too, was chronically ill.

Both situations rocked my heart, burdening me with a new challenge. How could I see this as growth? How could I respond to this with a most enlightened vibration rather than from a reaction of fear and tragedy? What could I do to help in healing? What was required of me in this moment?

Questions, questions, questions. The answers that came to me formed the basis of this book. I reviewed the principles that had helped me most in life, relying on the real truths that I drew from to get me through. I asked myself what I truly believed, what I held dear to the inner core of who I was, and what had worked to guide me thus far. I was again searching, this time for answers in a crisis. I found those answers, and I was further guided to share them.

We're all searching for answers. Why is it so complicated to recognize them when you find them? Why do you doubt what you instinctively know to be true? Why do you overthink and analyze answers that seem obvious? That's the nature of *unconscious* human behavior. That is not the nature of *conscious* spiritual behavior.

Awareness of the difference changes everything you do in life.

The question is, are we willing to wake up and recognize what we're doing? Fortunately, I woke up and my life now carries tremendous meaning. I am clearly on purpose. Several turning points catalyzed me into action.

While searching for guidance and a greater happiness, I excelled in my career, finding complete freedom in the creativity of television. I willingly moved myself from Washington, D.C., to Baltimore to Chicago to San Francisco to Los Angeles to New York to London as I moved up the ladder to the top rungs. I worked for Westinghouse Broadcasting, CBS, NBC, Lifetime Television, King World, Grant Tinker, David Letterman, Oprah Winfrey, and countless others. The road I traveled was fast—living in major cities, covering glamorous celebrities and fascinating topics.

Working for the networks and syndicated television was like mixing with a crew of gypsies—nomadic people who didn't cherish roots anywhere. That circle of acquaintances fed me in my early twenties up until age thirty-five, when nothing seemed to feel so nourishing anymore. The glamour no longer held much appeal, the dysfunction of spoiled celebrities seemed out of line, and the quest to earn a higher rating with some outlandish stunt seemed ridiculous.

I'll never forget sitting at Rockefeller Center, working for *Late Night with David Letterman,* assuming that by taking one of the hottest jobs in TV, I'd be happier than ever. I had landed at the esteemed NBC, working on the coolest show in America, and I hated it. Television had given me great experiences, taking me places I never would have seen otherwise. But it was time to move on. The players were always the same, the words had become clichés, and I was no longer interested in going through the same motions, just on a different show. Thank God I woke up.

The personal growth work I'd undertaken during that time was the main reason that television's allure no longer held me. The healthier I became, the less willing I was to spend fourteen-hour days amidst chaos. To separate from the commotion of 24/7 workdays, chain smoking, drinking, no personal life, and frantic deadlines, I chose to consult creatively and move into advertising in long-form commercials. Working with Kodak, Bristol-Myers, Maybelline, Lexus, Toyota, and others, I used my television skills to craft marketing messages. The transition to a saner environment, working in my own office, allowed me to continue working on my personal growth.

I began searching for spiritual answers. Drawing on my own Native American heritage, I found that a practice based on the principles of divine love and a belief in the unity of everything in life made sense. There was no hierarchy of humans above animals; there was an unbroken link between all beings—nature, animals, and people—and a cause-and-effect relationship between your actions today and your next life.

Various teachings helped shaped my consciousness. One goal was to wake up and embrace an awareness of how you are and what you do. Most of us "space out" because we learned long ago that in painful situations it's easier to be somewhere else. Exercises such as setting my wristwatch to beep every fifteen minutes taught me to stay present and to recognize how unfocused on the present I normally was. As soon as I heard the beep, I had to analyze how my thoughts had taken me into the past or future or elsewhere, definitely away from the moment at hand.

Another important teaching gave me a profound belief in God energy. It doesn't matter what you call the force of divine energy, the belief is what counts—knowing on a very profound level, through personal experiences, that God is with you every step of the way. With that understanding, I began a new healing. The first teachings had provided conscious awareness and clarity of who I was; the second provided a cocoon of support greater than myself. I even went to Frankfurt, Germany, to meet Mother Meera, a noted Avatar. In the eastern world, Avatars are people akin to Mother Teresa, people who are born completely in tune with God. There is no separation of spirit. They experience complete love and joy and are able to share that energy with others.

Synthesizing this growth in myself over the years led me to offer assistance to others as an intuitive coach. My own journey of transformation allowed me to see steps that others are taking or want to take and counsel them on how to proceed.

Individuals come to me because they want to have babies, land new work assignments, marry or divorce, improve their work life, or find more joy in living. I work with litigators, salespeople, television professionals, teachers, homemakers, real estate agents, writers, electricians, CEOs, marketing executives, computer experts—the list goes on. The one thing they all have in common is the desire to find some part of themselves that has been lost or hidden. They want to feel connected to a part of themselves creatively.

Many people work with me on a weekly basis, others every six weeks, and others whenever they find a need. Some work over years and others just come once or twice. I trust that if what I offer is helpful, they will know when I can be of help again. My main objective is to offer them freedom by sharing tools they can apply themselves without dependency on anyone else. This is what I offer in the *Little Book:* actual tools to put into practice to connect to your Soul.

In my own quest for freedom and contentment, I found that the longing for that inner connection is the link to your Soul. People don't always know that is what they are asking to find and, in fact, only a rare few start there. But by the time we finish working together, it's clear for them that it's their inner spirit, their Soul, that they want to invite into their life more fully.

Aside from healing my own pain, furthering my own awareness, and gaining greater consciousness, I deeply desired a committed love relationship. I knew on a very deep level that a real lifelong relationship would provide the greatest growth opportunity and healing of all. I worked diligently for two years to vision this person. Through various methods, I focused all my efforts on allowing him to arrive in my life. Creative scripting, energy healing, prayer, fear management—I'd use any tool that made sense to unblock obstacles to love. I knew my past had hardened my heart, so my present focus had to be strong and decisive. My own healing allowed the most generous, loving, incredible human being to join me every day. I had waited sixteen years for John, my true life partner. I wanted the blessing of as much time as possible together in this journey on Earth, which is why the possibility of losing him when he became so ill shook me so deeply.

The shift in my life has been dramatic. I've gone from the nomadic days of television to solo days of intensive healing and revelation to days spent with a partner, from whom I'm inseparable. We work together all the time, never apart more than a day. He has been the ultimate teacher of the heart, the place to test the corners that are still hidden, the foundation on which I can now stand. I trust his love as completely as I trust my place on this earth. A rock-solid connection, Soul to Soul.

For me, personally, teachers will never stop appearing in my life. I am committed and open to continued growth and greater connection to my Soul. The funny thing is that the form the teachers take has changed for sure: No longer on two legs teaching me with words, they now come on four legs with fur!

Soon after my partner and I found each other, we adopted our first dog, Luke, a Border collie. Abused and neglected, he cracked our hearts with his brave, gentle desire to reunite with humans. Luke had been a rescue dog, cast off to fend for himself. If a caring person hadn't committed to helping him, he would have died. I found myself drawn to the concept of rescue and helping this breed of dogs. Border collies are consummate workaholics. I identified with their intensity and need to do, do, do. Experiences with Luke, and soon other Border collies, prompted us to start Glen Highland Farm, where we foster 150 dogs a year, finding them new homes, using my intuitive skills to match dogs with people.

Little did I know that dogs would offer the greatest healing and teaching of all; they are excellent guides of the heart. The experience of being with so many unconditionally loving hearts, basically pure spirits, has profoundly impacted who I am. The dogs' wisdom embodies the principles in *The Little Book of Everyday Soul*. Unlike analytical humans, these dogs know their own spirits. All they want to do is share them with us. Forgiveness . . . love . . . simplicity . . . trust . . . relationship. They taught us all of these concepts and continue to do so, whenever in their presence. We sometimes think of them as Buddha dogs!

I write this now sitting on a porch of a hundred-year-old farmhouse in dairy country in upstate New York. We live on 183 acres of gorgeous countryside with a large roaring creek, an enchanting hemlock forest, a sixty-acre wide-sky meadow, and ten acres of paddocks for dogs to race and run and be free. People often think that since we made this decision, we must have loads of money, but the truth is very different. We have loads of trust in something greater than ourselves guiding us to this decision and to this land. We know that, in our hearts, the call to assist these dogs had to happen. Day to day, we wonder how the bills will be paid, but on a very deep level, we're able to release the fear and doubt.

How is it possible to really let go of fear and doubt? I focus on the present. I see the dogs racing wildly across acres and acres, released from their pain, and know that it's possible for humans to do this, too. The dogs don't worry about yesterday or tomorrow; they are teaching trust in today. So, we remain focused on today and being guided, moment by moment, toward whatever is next. Our Souls are in charge now.

So, as you read these words, know that life is a journey. I never expected in my wildest dreams to live in the middle of rolling hills and miles of farmland, listening to dozens of barking dogs playing in a sky-filled meadow, meeting new people who seek the heartfelt connection of a beloved dog. But what I do know is that if you want to connect to your Soul, you must ask for help. You must yearn for the connection and adjust your orientation to embody more spiritual principles. That's the purpose of this Little Book: to help you find your way. Each of us has different reasons for being here. It's our job to open the door to the answers.

CHAPTER ONE

Soulfulness

Sensing Your Soul

INSPIRATION
*That which you do not bring into consciousness
appears in our lives as fate.*

CARL JUNG

This chapter is about remembering. Remembering who you are, what you forgot, and why you continue to forget. The words here are meant to jog a deep part of your own wisdom, igniting your connection to your Soul. You've been led to believe that what you see tangibly around you is who you are. Now it's time to consider what you *sense and know*, not what you see and touch. This is the connection to your Soul.

At age thirty, I worked on the hottest entertainment show going. While that moment in time should have been the pinnacle of achievement for me, instead it felt like I'd been shipwrecked, sent adrift with a sea of misfits who were all whirling around with their own confused agendas. Everyone seemed busy enough and wore their workaholism like a badge of honor: "I work on *Late Night with David Letterman*." Yet somehow it always felt like I was on shaky ground, the house of cards surely on the verge of tumbling down. What was missing? Why was I in such pain, feeling so unhappy inside when everything outside looked so perfect? Because a part of me was disconnected—forgotten—not invited into my life. I'd successfully constructed the shell and forgotten what goes inside. It was this discontent that jarred me, literally, to my *senses* and triggered the searching that changed my life.

This Soul connection can guide you on a day-by-day basis, moment by moment, leading you to make decisions that are more fulfilling and nourishing, ultimately leading you to create a life that fits YOU.

If you wonder why your life goes haywire, why things seem chaotic and off course, or even if you wonder why there's no fun in it anymore, that's a sign that you, too, are disconnected from something important.

What you lack is the nourishing link to your Soul, your own *Soulfulness*.

You are not filled with anything of meaning, deep meaning. You may be busy, you may be successful, and some days, you may feel happy, but you are not fully nourished. And you know it. On some very deep level, you know you're being cheated. You can feel it. Usually, you cannot name it, but there is a nagging sense of something amiss, or a recurring voice in your head, reminding you that something needs to change. This is the innermost part of you, attempting to break through and get your attention. Attempting to wake you from the sleepwalk you call your life.

Have you ever felt this way? Really take a moment to think back in time.

Webster defines Soul as "the animating and vital principle in man, the spiritual nature of man, credited with the faculties of thought, action, and emotion and often conceived as an immaterial entity and regarded as immortal."

Century after century the meaning of this complex definition has eluded people. Thousands of books have been written, numerous religions offer guidance—and yet the search continues. That's because this is an individual search, not a formula where if you follow a, b, and c, you'll get a specific result.

The journey of the Soul is yours to take and yours alone. Are you brave enough?

Why the Soul Gets Lost

Imagine a small baby, full of infinite wisdom, fully capable with a knowledge so vast it would startle you. That's the truth of what each child brings into the world. We have incorrectly seen newborns as helpless, dependent, innocent, or uneducated because we've been seeing them through the wrong eyes. Just for a moment, imagine each baby coming into the world as a great teacher with something unique to share. What they have to offer is the information of the Soul. This infinitely rich, mysterious *Soulfulness* shapes everything they touch. But since we don't understand the wealth of wisdom *innate* in each child, we attempt to teach children everything they *need to know*. Like a quest for perfection, they are jammed with "real" information so they can become good citizens.

If we turned our assumptions upside-down, and instead saw our role as that of *facilitator*, in which we search for what *innately resonates* with the child, then children would shape their lives from the inside out, not from the outside in. Wise parents would know that their job is to nurture the wealth of information that already exists within their children, recognizing the wisdom of each child's Soul.

Which seems most nourishing? Being molded like a square peg for a square hole or being taught how to feel what fits for you, being taught how to sense your Soul's guidance . . . your Soulfulness?

Unfortunately, we're living in the Dark Ages. We may think we are advanced, but in reality we have beliefs that are old-fashioned and limiting. We barely allow something new to enter our mind-set because it makes us uncomfortable. So you can safely assume that your parents were *not* able to nurture your Soul. They did not recognize that you were born with a wealth of information. They did not attempt to discover what resonated with the deepest part of you. They did not assume you were infinitely wise and brilliant. They felt, as society told them, that you needed to be taught everything. You knew nothing and needed to learn everything. Does this make sense to you given the childhood you experienced?

Soulfulness is about unlearning that lie.
Unlearning the beliefs that are limiting you.
Unlearning the rules of "what is."
Opening to a new way, a recognition of a deep level of "knowing."

Take the first step in believing that you are brilliant, that you have a guidance system that can work perfectly if you'd only find it and trust it. Can you do that?

The only difference between the baby and us as mature full-grown people is that we've added layers and layers and layers of knowledge on top of that pure wisdom. These learned layers are thick crusts distorting reality. We've added information to define who we are, forgetting what we already knew. This focus on the layers has taken us away from our birth information. After many years, we've actually forgotten our *sense* of our Soul. It's been buried.

Like a fingerprint, the individual Soul is unique to each one of us. And, it's the Soul's guidance that we are longing to hear. It's what makes the search so worthwhile. Your life's work is to uncover the connection to your Soul. *And, to listen.*

The good news is that your Soul is always available to you. No matter what terror you lived in childhood or how awful your behavior as an adult, your Soul does not leave you. There has and always will be an opportunity to find this essential part of yourself. A commitment to search for Soulfulness is the key.

Many successful clients ask for my assistance in realigning their lives. They've reached a point of success or failure (which are actually very similar experiences) and they are no longer content. Something must change. Of course, they initially apply the learned behavior of control and attempt to force a change, take charge of the moment, and make something happen. But, each and every time, what's really required is less action and more searching. The pain or confusion is actually a wake-up call to connect to their own Souls, going beyond the mind and deep into the heart.

Listen to Your Heart, Not Your Mind

The opportunity to live from the Soul is possible for each of us. All that is required is an openness to learning—that is, *re*-learning.

> *A switch from the mind to the heart.*
> *An ability to listen, inside yourself.*

Your heart is the link to your Soul. The capacity you have to feel, to love, to know others is how you find joy and meaning in your life. It is also how you hear your Soul's guidance.

The Soul can only be heard in silence. Once you know your own stillness, rhythm, pace, and way of hearing, you will know the Soul's guidance everywhere and at all times. You have then welcomed the Soul as the guiding principle of how you live on this planet. Nothing can overshadow the clarity of knowing inherent in this connection.

If you are committed to glamour, owning things, and making money, then it is harder to hear your Soul's guidance. There are too many distractions in the way. If you are committed to obligations, hardship, and carrying burdens, then the link to your Soul is hidden. There is too much bitterness in the way. If you are committed to deadlines, busyness, and schedules, then there is no time for your Soul. There is too much noise stifling the Soul's call to you.

The process of finding your Soul—caring for and feeding it, as many bestsellers say—is not that difficult. You only make it that way. Once you focus on the journey to know your Soul, you will attract experiences that do just that. This is a spiritual principle.

Remember, though, that you may not perceive those experiences as positive. This is why it's important to shift into a relearning mode. Let go of what you hold as positive and negative. Stop looking to outer results.

You are looking inside now. You are attempting to reorient your life on a Soulful level. What you think may be "good" for you may not be after all.

Learning, as a priority in life, is critical. Because whatever we think we know, must be challenged. That is the nature of Soulfulness. When you are "full of Soul," there is no room for beliefs based on past limitations. There is no room for prejudiced, egotistical judgments. Letting go of the "important" knowledge you possess makes room for real knowing, the deep knowing of the Soul. If you want a connection to your Soul, you will have to live in a learning mode.

A client came to me with her issues about her boss. She found that, over and over again, his comments about her work enraged her. He seemed so caustic, callous, and discouraging. She got so disoriented and upset that she had a harder time staying motivated to work. No matter how she interacted with her boss, she felt so overly sensitive that she knew it negatively influenced his opinion of her. Unbeknownst to her, her boss had also come to me with the same issue. Her emotional reactions created a roller-coaster relationship that was making him quite weary. In fact, her career was in jeopardy.

Rather than focus on her boss and his approach to her, I asked her to focus on herself and the underlying reactions that he triggered. We went back in time to the earliest experience where she had been judged harshly. In her case, it had been her stepfather, a man who joined the family in her youth and then began to critique her every move. She felt smothered, unable to be herself. As we dug deeper, she realized that his disapproval had had a tremendous impact on her ability to trust her own judgment. She was critical of herself, even before someone spoke. She anticipated her failures before they happened. And she was tremendously anxious about not being "good enough."

Over the next few weeks, she began to focus on the opportunity presented to her by this work situation. It really had very little to do with her boss and mostly to do with a part of herself that had never been healed. In fact, she'd done very little work to understand her pain. Soon she began to see what she could learn. She actually transformed her pain into a chance to understand her feelings about her stepfather. She saw every interaction as a way to gain information about what she'd hidden for so long.

This approach to handling pain can accelerate your growth. You shift into a learning mode to unearth the pain and release it. The healing is in the release, which then frees pent-up energy. You then have more freedom to explore your own inner guidance, which is how you connect with your Soul.

Are you ready to learn again?

Soulful living involves personal development, a commitment to growth as the key priority in all decisions. The assumptions you make about yourself are evolutionary in nature, not fixed one way forever. You are digging for the truth, searching for clarity, and ruthless about changing whatever is false, no matter why it exists. You can expect change. You learn to welcome it.

Why is personal development related to the Soul? Because the odds are that you have stopped growing, stopped learning.

At a certain age, you are mechanically living a recurring pattern of activities. Some people call it a "rut," others say their life is predictable. If you're like most people, you've grown up, learned some skills, feel accomplished in some areas, and have a pretty strong sense of what you like and don't like. You are, more or less, set in your ways. Some people have actually described this to me as feeling "dead." They are, in fact, describing the sensation correctly. A part of themselves has been deadened, put to sleep, forgotten, in order to exist. They can no longer hear that deep wealth of information available from the Soul.

A Snapshot—The Soul Knocking at Your Door

At forty-five, Bill (not his real name) had attained his idea of success: a loving family, two children, a nice home in a well-to-do suburb of a major East Coast city, and a ten-year career as a highly paid lawyer. From the outside looking in, he had what most people strive to attain. And, in fact, he had been satisfied with his progress for the first five years. But the last five had been stifling, unsettling, and for some reason unknown to him, much less fulfilling. He came to me perplexed. Everyone told him he must be crazy for contemplating a change. Even his wife couldn't understand what was bothering him. He felt guilty for even admitting his unhappiness. He apologized countless times for being so unclear about what was bothering him. His first consultation was a mixture of confused emotions and, finally, his acceptance that being unhappy was a real message that could not be ignored.

Bill was lucky. He chose to wade through the confusion, *searching* for something that he was not even sure he would find. There were no guarantees. He had no way of knowing what outcome lay ahead. The one thing he did know was that he had to open the door to search. As we worked together in weekly sessions, he began to learn what *resonated* with him and what did not. Not what was good for him, what was "right," or what he should like or want, but what *resonated* with him. Learning to sense when something resonated with him gave him new confidence. He began to unlock something hidden inside himself. He began to unlock his creativity, his intuition, and his own *knowing*. At the time I knew he was listening to his Soul, but it was still too early to explain this to him. That would come later.

Bill was a quick study. He had trusted his intuition years ago and, in fact, his former business had relied on it. But the legal world had negated it, relying instead on facts and linear thinking. As each year rolled by, he was happy to take the money, but felt that a part of him was unutilized and dying. It was that inner part that had begun to call out to him and create his discontent.

When you stifle an innate part of who you are (your Soulfulness), you will feel dampened, boxed in, less alive. Eventually, the call to wake up and acknowledge this part of yourself that needs to be expressed will grow so loud that you must make a change. Or, with avoidance, you will attract an illness or tragedy, forcing you to make the change.

Fortunately, Bill chose to act. He committed himself to challenging every aspect of his decision making in search of his inner voice, his inner sense of what best fit him. That meant examining his relationships, his business interactions, his environment, and even his future. It was his future that scared him the most. Questions like: How can I make any changes? What will happen if I do? How can I be sure it will work out? How do I keep everyone happy? Will everything fall apart if I follow this inner guidance? Bill began to feel his own information, his own answers to what was needed, but he was fearful of trusting them.

Welcoming the Soul

In the field of intuitive coaching, there are never assurances you can offer to any client that life will remain "happy and safe." This is not what the Call of the Soul is about. A safe, happy life is generally a deadened life, without growth, without resonance. When clients tell me they aren't sure what is wrong, but that something isn't right, I know they will experience change, that a transition lies ahead.

We are meant to resonate with the earth and everything around us. Can you remember a time when you knew that? Maybe as a child? Or as an adult?

One simple way to illustrate this is to imagine a vacation experience. When you travel away to someplace in nature, away from urban life—the ocean, camping, sailing, hiking—and you allow yourself to experience a different rhythm, you begin to feel relief. It's as if you decompress. There is room for you to breathe, laugh, sleep, daydream—basically just be. You come into resonance with nature.

This pace and rhythm are not what most people experience in daily life, commuting for many hours, working in concrete settings with artificial lighting and piped-in air, phones ringing, and the pressure of deadlines. It's impossible to resonate with chaos, yet that's what most people do. They train themselves to think that is "normal." But it is not natural in any shape or form, which is what causes the dissonance deep inside. You are totally out of sync with your inner self.

So not only has your upbringing buried your connection to that inner information, but you then create a daily life that buries it further. It's as if you have piled thousands upon thousands of bricks on top of your body—and then wondered why you don't feel right. Everything you came into this world already knowing as a baby has been buried deep underground, with no tools to access it. That beautiful innate stuff of which you are made—the Soul—is left untapped, unknown, literally buried alive.

> *Your Soul connects to the stuff of the earth. Relearning that pace, rhythm, and freedom allows you to hear the guidance of the Soul.*

It's the voice inside tapping ever so slightly on your conscious awareness, growing louder until you finally notice.

For Bill, he realized he'd wasted five years denying that anything was wrong. Now he had to search for this new life. Now it was critical to sustain himself, from the *inside out*. It had actually become painful to pretend he could continue "as normal" in the life he had created.

What happened to Bill had happened to me at age thirty. Looking back sixteen years, I can tell you with complete confidence that the pain of that time was the greatest blessing. Cracking open the seemingly "successful" life led me to land so fully in my heart, knowing my own Soul that I will always be grateful I had the courage to begin the search and keep on searching. The search is a long, fruitful journey that continues to be *the* most important point to living. There is no other reason for being here except to find this inner link to your own wisdom. It is your birthright. It is why you are here. But only you can choose to be truly open.

A courageous life is one lived following guidance from the Soul.

> *Once you learn to see all situations around you as opportunities for personal growth and stay open to learning, you will then be in communication with your Soul. The rich inner world of YOU is then yours to tap.*

Most of us have little understanding of how to invite communication with the Soul. Yet, in reality, we know exactly how to do this. *If we listen carefully to all the times we "feel" what we "should do" but don't do it, or we "know" the better answer but don't trust it, we'll know that the Soul has always been offering an option.* We were the ones who blocked the information.

> *The commitment to personal growth will lead you directly to the search for your Soul.*

The two are linked. If you choose the deepest level of living, you will accept the inner world of your Soul as the guiding principle.

What follows in *The Little Book of Everyday Soul* is meant to guide you to Soulfulness. Each chapter offers a key to unlocking a new way of living.

CHECKPOINTS: *Where Are You Now?*

- What relationship do you have with your Soul now?
- What commitment are you willing to make to yourself to explore this connection?
- How open is your heart?
- Are you willing to stop knowing and begin learning again?
- Are you brave enough to admit you don't know?
- As a way of understanding how clearly you now focus on your Soul, honestly answer a few more questions:

   How do you now make decisions in your life?

   How often do you procrastinate or deny that you need to change something?

   How long have you felt a sense that something is missing in your life but don't know what it is?

   How many times do you sit quietly alone, without thinking?

Principles for Reflection

Work with these principles:

- *Soulfulness is about unlearning the beliefs that are limiting you, opening to a new way, a recognition of a deep level of "knowing."*

- *Focus on making a switch from the mind to the heart. Your heart is the link to your Soul.*

- *The Soul can only be heard in silence.*

- *You are looking inside now.*

- *The Soul connects to the stuff of the earth.*

- *Once you learn to see all situations around you as opportunities for personal growth and stay open to learning, you will then be in communication with your Soul. The rich inner world of YOU is then yours to tap.*

Love
The Energy of Love

The truth of your Soul lies in your heart, not in your mind or your body. Your heart will not lie. So, why do we so frequently ignore our hearts? Why do we distrust and fear where our hearts will lead us? Why are we so unaware of how to follow our hearts? If we don't find the answers, we're condemned to live a life without the rewards of love.

I sit writing about love surrounded by seven of my eleven dogs plus a seven-week-old rescue pup, all lying comfortably on the couch, the floor—basically wherever they like. These dogs share incredible wisdom on this topic. I start with them as a frame of reference because . . .

It's so important to understand that love is something you cannot do to yourself, by yourself. You must engage in the energy of love with some other being, whether human, animal, or in nature. Love is an energy that is exchanged.

Your heart is meant to be open, to give and receive love. The benefit of receiving the kind of "innocent love" that results from a connection with an animal is that you cannot reason your way through the experience. The dog, cat, or other animal simply *is* love. Animals naturally share their love; they surround you with unconditional adoration. And they never stop offering their love.

Animals give us the truth about love: what it is, how it works, and, most important, how good it feels.

The phrase "in love" accurately describes the bliss of this energy. When we "fall out of love," that is literally what we are doing: leaving that energy.

Though it's sometimes difficult to see from within the concrete cities we live in, there are infinite ways to experience the energy of love. Wander along a creek, lie in the sunshine, watch birds soar, or let yourself be nibbled on by a puppy—that energy is love. Your heart feels it and naturally responds by expanding to allow room for more love to enter. In letting down your guard, you feel a huge sense of relief. You begin soaking in the sensation of joy. You are being nourished, just by the energy of love. Incredible moments of love can occur while you're alone if you open yourself up to its energy.

That is the entire point.

Rather than looking at love as something related to a partner, a person to commit to, look at love as an energy you want to bring into your life more fully.

Just as you might start a fitness regimen, imagine a program designed to encourage "love moments"—as many as you can possibly bring into each day.

Wouldn't that goal bring more satisfaction than counting calories in pursuit of the leanest body? Of course it would because love, as energy, is *the* most nourishing, satisfying food for the heart, mind, body, *and* Soul.

If you decide that the energy of love is worthy of your attention, and that you want more of it in your life, then you will naturally lead a more Soulful life. Your pursuits will naturally involve only those activities that bring you love. You will cast off the nonsense of analytical second-guessing, idle chitchat, and wasted interactions. If bringing love into your life is your goal, you just won't bother with anything that detracts from achieving that goal. If something or someone is not nourishing you with love, then you will not permit that activity or that person in your life.

That's exactly what happened to me. After a few years of hard work on my personal issues, I knew that while I'd made great progress in healing wounds, my heart was still closed. I knew that opening my heart to feel again was the only thing that mattered. If I could allow that to happen, everything else would naturally flow from that change. I decided that love would be my focus, my entire focus.

Anyone who focuses intensely on something knows that once you apply your energy in a certain direction, things move and change. It's impossible for change *not* to happen. But the reason many people achieve such scattered results is because they don't know how to hold their focus. Once you truly focus your energy, you will attract what's needed.

To understand focus and intention, think of an athlete who trains day in and day out, sharply tuning her mind and body in a singular direction. Whether the focus is running, tennis, or something else, the athlete is focused on one thing—not lots of things. Great coaches will always tell you that winning is a *mind* game: It all has to do with how you direct your thoughts. That's true with *everything* in life. Scattered thoughts do not bring focused results.

With love, you must focus on allowing it into your life. If you say you want a partner and long for that important relationship, then at another time speak of how you cherish your time alone and fear a partner's intrusion and the needs of a committed relationship, it's very hard to achieve either.

One of my clients came to me years ago, desiring a serious relationship. She was a professional woman in her early thirties who had dated a few men but had not found a compatible partner. We worked together for close to six months trying to keep her energy focused on love. Each week, she expressed different reasons she was afraid of having a serious partner and a consuming relationship. Yet she felt defeated that she had not found someone yet. Helping her understand her conflicting signals was the beginning of helping her refocus.

Energy that is clearly focused allows you to attract and receive what you say you want.

But if what you say you want changes all the time? What you want will not happen. It's a lot like a fuzzy radio signal: You can't hear the music or words clearly. You're exactly the same way. Desires that are clear one day and fuzzy the next create scattered results. That is a principle of energy and how it works.

For myself, I knew how to set an intention and focus, but I also knew I was afraid of love. I knew I'd need extra assistance. I knew that my fear might cause me to waver. That's where a spiritual connection can help. I prayed. It didn't matter to me what God was or wasn't; it only mattered that I asked for assistance from a higher, infinitely wiser energy, one that could miraculously help in ways I'd never expect. To me, God is not the religious, punishing figure we've often feared. Instead, God represents a higher power, a divine source of universal life energy that is naturally a part of who we are. I prayed for the healing of my heart. I focused nonstop on my longing to connect with the energy of love, to really know my heart and be guided by love. I truly wanted to heal the obstacles preventing me from knowing love, and I prayed with every cell of my body for assistance to do just that. On some very deep level, I knew that my ability to be "in love" would change my life, finally grounding me in a fulfilling way. What I sensed was that my destiny could finally become real.

I didn't know much about love, but I knew I didn't have it. I thought I could give it, but I had not had the chance to experience true love, the love I sensed was possible. Then it became clear in a meditation one day. Two pictures of myself emerged to help me understand how I could achieve what I longed for. With love, I saw people all around, me laughing happily. Without love, I saw myself as a bitter, crusty old woman alone in an apartment. That meditation was a rude awakening to a choice that only I could make: Choose love or suffer without it.

Love Is the Most Important Focus

We're all damaged by life—hurtful parents, difficult siblings, uncaring people who make caustic remarks. We can all uncover where the pain still lives.

The truth is that the only way out is through your heart.

An interesting fact emerges when you work with animals in need, like the dogs we rescue at our farm. Most come to us, neglected and abandoned, distrusting humans. Some avoid being touched for fear of a painful interaction; others cower, slowly crawling forward toward an outstretched hand, hoping for kindness, yet fearful. The dogs' reactions are similar to the way people react when they've been hurt. The big difference is this: Dogs don't make overriding decisions to block out love, determined never to feel pain. They don't create obstacles, closing down their ability to feel from their hearts. They don't stop the flow. And they don't become bitter, losing hope that someone will love them. That's what humans do. We consciously make decisions to prevent pain, closing down our hearts in the process.

*The truth is if you value the energy of love, you must
CONSCIOUSLY open your heart to someone, something,
or some experience. You need another being for the energy
to flow. You must be willing to feel from your heart, not
your head.*

The dogs have taught me so much about love. They came
into my life as part of that deep longing and prayer when I
called out for healing. It was the higher intelligence, which
some may call God, that sent the dogs to me. Rather than rely
on another person to show me love, I relied on an unseen
energy to teach me how to allow love into my life. I felt my way
through, craving more and more moments of love energy
during which I felt deliciously alive. And the dogs gladly shared
what they innately knew.

They were love. Even in their fear they reached out to me,
asking to exchange love and share our hearts. They never ana-
lyzed or second-guessed themselves; they never worried that
knowing me would be painful. They just came closer and
closer, and the more I opened my heart to them, the more they
opened theirs to me. Together we energetically found each
other and the love flowed. Almost 200 dogs have given themselves to me, as I have given myself to them, because both dogs
and human knew the healing power of that energy.

It is unusual to be surrounded by so much love given so freely and unconditionally. The impact is dramatic because the human world doesn't operate this openly. We are guarded, careful, and afraid. If, as humans, we could exchange love as freely as animals do, we would all be quickly healed.

Take, for example, an interesting program in prisons that allows select inmates to foster puppies to be service dogs in the community. Inmates care for and love the pups for months within the prison, having earned the privilege of participating in the program. The transformation of the participants is proof positive of the power of exchanging love energy. The pups know no harm, only giving their full unconditional love without judgment. The inmates naturally open their hearts to respond with love, healing some of their own pain, changing them in a positive way.

Love's power is energy, a healing energy. You want to allow this sensation into your life, regardless of how it comes.

Many women who come to me for coaching, as well as my friends, are searching for the love of their lives. They long for a partner to understand them, nourish them, and be forever theirs. They feel their lives would be fuller if their true loves appeared. There is truth in this longing because on a deep level they know that they could experience more love if the right partner came along. But there is fantasy here, too. Many times they are focusing on a single person as the source of the love when, in fact, the energy of love comes from everything around them. The more they open their hearts to the energy of love, the more likely it is that a loving person can find them.

A wise teacher once told me that our sense of feeling love from another can only be a reflection of our own capacity to love. A person can love someone else with all his or her energy, yet if the other person won't let it in, he or she cannot feel it.

Become a Seeker of Love

Allowing love to fully embody your life is a process. If you knew you could have love fully, you would already have it. So part of the process is unlearning the lie that you cannot and do not deserve love. This takes time. Count all the little victories, not just the obvious big ones—like finding the perfect life partner. That counts and counts big, but the everyday "in love" moments also change who you are and shape what your life will become. And that all adds up to a more Soulful life.

So much as been written about love, so many songs sung, so many stories told—and yet we know very little about how to live with our heart *leading* the way. That's actually what love is, even if it doesn't seem to make logical sense. Your heart *leads;* it does not follow. We are most comfortable letting our minds choose what's best, not *feeling* what really brings us joy. In fact, we talk ourselves out of the sensation of joy. We rationalize the right thing to do. We actually learn to doubt our hearts, block the sensations that come from them, and deny their wisdom.

A life lived every day with Soul requires that you abandon deadened patterns to reconnect deep within yourself, to your joy, your life's energy, and your passion.

In asking to be "in love," the most important thing to remember is to receive whatever comes to you with grace.

The pursuit of love in your life is about fully being alive. Your Soul is the guiding force, leading you to create your life. Your heart is the key to hearing that guidance. It's that simple.

If each of us spent time at school learning the meaning behind this simple sentence, we would have such insight into ourselves. We would create a happiness far greater than we could ever imagine. The unfortunate truth is that formal education—as well as informal education—focuses on facts, rules, and proven knowledge. The ability to regurgitate this information is considered a mark of intelligence. Yet the intelligence and wisdom of the heart is never studied, rarely mentioned.

The irony is that as a child, your heart was in full operation, clearly in charge, and giving signals about what made you happy and what made you sad. The observant adult might say that children are naive, unburdened by "real life," which allows for their happiness. That explanation may seem accurate, except it's really describing a change in focus—the analytical side of you begins to take control, forcing the heart into the background. You are conditioned to block your heart's wishes and rely on your mind for reasoning and deduction. Adults worry, overthink, fear, seek approval, and distrust themselves, whereas children have no such hang-ups. They act from their hearts based on what feels right in the moment. Living a more Soulful life requires that you return to your heart and what feels right in the moment. In essence, the child in you comes back to life, trusting that love is possible.

Reading about love if your heart isn't open is akin to reading a history textbook where you feel a bit removed from the events: It's something untouchable and distant, yet supposedly real.

Your capacity to experience your heart impacts your ability to feel love from another. The more you allow yourself to feel the energy of love, from whatever source you find, the more fully you can feel love.

The more you are around this energy, the more you will live from your heart. Remember, it's not about a particular person loving you, it's about feeling joy.

The "great love" is what women often talk about and dream of—that one person who will join your life and forever change you for the better. I found that partner after two years of focusing on love, committed to opening my heart. Fully aware that I had been hurt and shut down my heart before, I walked bravely toward another love experience. This time, the difference was that I accepted the person as a teacher, someone who could give me greater practice allowing the energy of love into my life. No promises about the result—just practice healing myself in order to love even more.

This orientation of practice, not perfection, of receiving each person as an opportunity to learn about love and heal whatever is hurt, gives you permission to explore. Just like the dogs that are afraid yet seek affection, you can learn to trust love again, moment by moment. Do not focus on the result;

focus on the growth of learning what love energy is and how you feel receiving it. Change your orientation to be a seeker of love, committed to opening your heart and making room for your Soul to guide you. Remember: Your Soul works through your heart.

Love everything—yourself, your friends, your animals, your home, your art, your food, your time off, your time working. Love is worth striving for.

NEVER give up on love. Never long for love without taking the steps necessary to invite it into your life. Go out on a limb and find it. Risk everything to open your heart. Move to another state if you have to, save animals from a shelter, have all the sex you want, change your name and start over. . . .

Do anything and everything to discover your heart.

Love is who you are, period. Love is what you deserve. Love is the reason you are here. This is not fantasy love—this is deep from your heart and gut and Soul love, of the earth and trees and sun love.

Breathe in the sun. Bake in the heat. Let your cheeks tingle in the warmth. Really go to the sensation of receiving. That is LOVE.

Let your heart lead.

This is simple stuff. Love in every moment is the answer.

Stop focusing on success. Stop arguing about who did you in. Stop holding your love for someone special. Love everything. Love yourself.

Start where you are right now. Find one thing about yourself and love that.

People I counsel find it difficult to open their hearts because they waste so much energy focused on what's wrong with them and so little time on loving themselves. They miss the opportunities to feel love.

Do whatever it takes to open your heart to love and loving. There is no other reason to be alive.

CHECKPOINTS: *Where Are You Now?*

- Who do you love?
- How are you loved?
- When do you create love?
- What's in the way?
- What are you willing to change?

Principles for Reflection

Work with these principles:

- *Love is something you cannot do to yourself, by yourself. You must engage in the energy of love with some other being, whether it's human, animal, or in nature. Love is an energy that is exchanged.*

- *Rather than looking at love as something related to a partner, a person to commit your life to, look at love as an energy you want to bring into your life more fully.*

- *Energy that is clearly focused allows you to attract and receive what you say you want.*

- *Think of what you do easily, what requires little effort, and what you are rewarded for over and over again. This is your natural excellence.*

- *The truth is if you value the energy of love, you must CONSCIOUSLY open your heart to someone, something, or some experience. You need another being for the energy to flow. You must be willing to feel from your heart, not your head.*

- *Your capacity to experience your heart impacts your ability to feel love from another. The more you allow yourself to feel the energy of love, from whatever source you find, the more fully you can feel love.*

- *In asking to be "in love," the most important thing to remember is to receive whatever comes to you with grace.*

- *Do anything and everything to discover your heart.*

CHAPTER THREE

KNOWING
The Wisdom of What You Know

INSPIRATION

The only tyrant I accept in this world is the still voice within.

MAHATMA GANDHI

Living a life connected to your Soul every day comes from one key ability: having a sense of knowing. When you think of the skills that you utilize in life, some are more important than others. An open heart is at the top of the list, as is knowing, yet most of us have very little understanding of what this even means.

The ability to know is the most important innate talent you can ever develop.

Living a life without this skill is like being in a boat without a rudder, drifting whichever way the waves move. For many people, this accurately describes the way their lives happen. But there is another way to *create* your life. You can develop and sharpen your capacity *to know*.

Knowing is an alive state of being very different from having knowledge. It is not about learning from books and teachers.

Knowing describes your innate inner sense of what is right for you, what fits and what does not.

Something like a divining rod, your own knowing, when accessed, gives you complete guidance about everything. Rather than using your analytical skills to help you make decisions, you rely on knowing. This approach is very foreign to most westerners and requires you to retrain yourself to a more natural way of knowing what you know, not what you think you know or *should* know.

This level of knowing comes from your heart.

The depth of who you are lives inside the openness of your heart. When you live connected to your heart, what you feel, sense, and trust is centered in spirit. There is no need for outer noise, interference of others, or fear. Each step in life leads you to greater knowing from your heart.

Remember, you don't need an education to be smart. You don't need to be an adult to be smart. You don't need a good job to be smart. You enter this world with complete knowing in every cell of your being.

> *You are gifted with extreme intelligence the very day you are born.*

This infinite wisdom is what makes your body work without much help from you, makes the trees and flowers grow without much help from you, makes the sun rise and moon shine without much help from you. . . . Getting the picture? There is an inner wisdom in you, just like everything else you see around you. The flower receives energetic guidance and knows how to use it. It doesn't ask itself, "Am I the right flower?" It just knows what is needed, receiving and responding with ease. You have the same capacity.

> *You have simply forgotten what you already know and you are in pursuit of what you think you're supposed to know.*

Trusting Yourself

The closest experience most of us have to inner "knowing" is intuition. It's that sense of knowing something that cannot logically be explained. You just "know" if something is right to do, if someone is "off," or if you need to be in a certain place, for example. Everyday situations present opportunities for you to sense or know all the time. There are countless examples if you stop and think about them. A woman I met at a speaking event told me that once, when she heard the doorbell ring, for some reason she couldn't even explain, she knew to lock the screen door before she opened fully the inner door to the house. She averted a robbery right on the spot. Another woman told me she was in the middle of the "perfect" job interview. Everything seemed to be exactly what she wanted—the right salary, a noted company, a great title, and even flexible hours. Yet, for some reason she just couldn't put her finger on, she just knew to say no. Later, she learned that the boss she would have worked for was notorious for emotionally abusing employees. A man I once worked with told me he'd met his wife only once at a social event, and he just knew he would marry her. Again, he could not articulate how he knew, but he just knew.

Knowing accesses a part of you that is *always* available to provide guidance. Most of the time you ignore what you're sensing, or you are so busy that you cannot even connect to anything other than what your head tells you is so.

Yet, if you practice trusting information that comes from deep within you, you strengthen your ability to know all the time.

It's not just an occasional experience; it's constant, which means that you are more connected to your Soul, receiving guidance that is best for you.

The only reason you doubt "knowing" in this way is that you have not practiced and trusted the experience of listening inside yourself. No one told you this was possible. One way to understand how you know what you know is this: Think of yourself as if you were a computer. When you were a baby, you had your own hard drive, but everyone assumed that wasn't the case, so they began giving you lots of software with all kinds of programming. Others gave you everything they thought you needed to know; they programmed your hard drive according to their own beliefs. Rarely did anyone check to see what you might already innately know. Year after year this went on. You learned everything you needed to know to live on the planet.

Trouble is, no one told you that at some point, a nagging inner voice would pop up, testing you with unanswered questions, giving you guidance without asking. No one helped you understand your own knowing, your own intuitive nature. Instead, they told you what you should do, what would be best for you. No one told you that answers already existed within you and that all you had to do was tap into your own inner information. If you'd known this, how differently would you be making decisions today?

The Signal for Change

For many people, the time comes when the inner and outer world conflict. A seemingly perfect life falls apart. Unrest occurs. All is not well. Something just isn't working quite as it should. The life that the person has built doesn't fit the person living it. While this doesn't mean you throw everything away and start over, it does mean that an inner part of you is desperately trying to be expressed. A deep part of you, connected to your Soul, is craving change. Whether acknowledged or not, this guidance grows and grows, attempting to move you to listen to your heart, taking action to satisfy your longing. You are being asked to be true to your inner self, not the outer one you've attempted to build.

A client came to me after leaving his family business. For fifteen years, he'd successfully built a division he could be proud of, but in the last few years a strong sense that he should move on had disturbed him. He kept feeling he didn't belong there any longer, that it wasn't the right place for him to be. He battled that inner information until he became severely ill with heart palpitations, dizziness, and exhaustion. A doctor persuaded him to break away from his current work—it was killing him. This man in his late thirties faced what most people strive to avoid—a point in his life when the outer world no longer worked. He had to find a new way. The good news for him was that he started with his intuition. Rather than jump into another profession, he took a six-month sabbatical, spending time to uncover what he loved in life, what gave him joy. This quieter time of reflection and searching provided him with a way to hear his inner knowing more clearly. Then he could re-create his life, from the inside out.

The process of shifting from outer pressures to inner reliance will not happen overnight. It takes time—months and years—before you realize that you have the courage to shape a life around what's best for you. Remember that you've spent at least twenty-plus years convincing yourself you knew what was best, without ever listening intently inside to your own guidance. You soaked up outside information as if it was your own. The shift to listening inside is initially uncomfortable, yet ultimately invigorating.

As this man spent time in sessions, uncovering his joy, he began to realize that at the young age of nine, he consciously decided he could not pursue any creative work. He had won an art contest and, while everyone was proud of him, some other message sunk in: "That's not how you make a living." He pushed his desire for art further away from his reality. So when he was offered a place in his father's business, he took it. Away went his own sense of what felt interesting, satisfying, and fulfilling. Fifteen years later, he has now rented a small space in an artist's building where he's begun painting. Never trained as an artist, he's exploded onto canvas, painting literally hundreds of pieces—deep, bold colors, swaths of color moving in circles, vivid impressions of movement. His abstract work has been shown at community events and he's begun to sell to people he knows. His most important comment to me: "No one will ever take my creativity away again."

Just imagine if the young boy had been encouraged. Imagine if those around him had nurtured that inner creativity. Where would he have been if his adult life had been devoted to artistic work? One thing is for sure, he would have been completely reliant on a *deep knowing* developed year after year as he created the life he truly wanted.

Stillness Leads to Answers

To rekindle this innate inner knowing, you need silence and a commitment to listening.

In quiet, you can practice tuning inside, asking questions, and receiving answers. The stillness assists you in hearing your own inner language. Access to a quiet moment comes in nature with a simple focus of listening to birds or wind in the trees, feeling the sun on your face—tuning in with the senses. Or it can happen in a city environment where you focus on your breathing, tuning out everything else.

The rhythm of your breathing is the rhythm of nature. It's an involuntary action. It just is. This is the rhythm you want to tap into; it gives you access to your own information. Breathing calms the body, allowing you to let go of extraneous thoughts so you can "tune" inside. Breathing also nourishes the body and mind so you can be more alert. Lastly, breathing stills the emotions so you can remove unnecessary feelings that may block your ability to hear from inside yourself.

When you are balanced, guidance about decisions and anything in life can come forward. When you're in chaos, it's impossible to hear much of anything, and that is when you analyze and "figure out" what to do, rather than tune inside yourself.

One client always came to me with the same busy energy that filled her day. She was a high-powered sales executive working in the Internet business, where decision making happens at the speed of light, 24/7. She initially came to me seeking balance in her life. She felt unnourished and less content than she wanted to be. As she sat at the table, she smoked and spoke so fast, it was tiring to be with her. Two years later, this same woman is calm, thoughtful, and less rushed. She learned the value of slowing everything down to match her inner rhythm. While she still works in a fast-paced job, she knows what works with her rhythm and what does not. Her entire journey discovering the richness of her inner being all started with her breath. *She had to learn to breathe again.*

While it sounds so simple, breathing requires practice. We no longer know how to breathe to nourish the body, so we shallow breathe. Everything is rushed, including our breathing.

Just take a moment and breathe deeply now, from your toes up to your lungs. Really bring the oxygen in, consciously filling your body. Give your body what it is craving. Feed yourself. If you try this now, for a few breaths, you'll begin to feel the difference. Breathe a few sequences, focused on just your breath. Your entire body will release, let go of the tension, and you'll begin to feel calmer. If you keep doing this, you'll begin to feel energized and clearheaded. Stay focused on your breath only, no thoughts. Closing your eyes can be helpful. When you focus on your own breath, you are focusing inside yourself. Your awareness of the inner you increases.

Tuning into the inner "vault" inside you is what allows you to "know." Your breath unlocks that knowing so you can begin to release all the outer interference.

Once you are practiced in breathing and feeling your rhythm, you can begin to ask for guidance. Rather than asking a friend or a relative, pose the question to *yourself*.

Remember that you have valuable wisdom inside. *All you have to do is ask.*

When you're starting out, reversing the listening from outside to inside, it's helpful to create a time for quiet. You may consider a ritual of sorts, where you know you have time to sit quietly, breathing, calming yourself, letting go of thoughts. When you focus on your breath, you will naturally release the random thoughts that flood your mind all day long. The goal is to train yourself to create a calm "center," a state of being that quiets outer noise so you can finally hear yourself. Some may refer to this as meditation, but it doesn't matter what it's called, the important point is to find a quiet stillness within yourself so you can begin a dialogue to uncover your own knowing.

Sometimes answers come in pictures. Sometimes answers come in everything you "coincidentally" encounter. And sometimes answers come over time, like a mosaic with pieces fitting together one by one to make the artwork complete. The language of inner wisdom is the language of the Soul, which has a grace, in being, that we must first learn.

If you're facing a dilemma or situation where you need more clarity, create some time for stillness and then begin to ask questions:

- What am I not seeing here?
- What do I need to know now?
- What is best for my highest good? My greatest growth?
- What does my heart want? What does my heart feel?

No matter what question you ask, begin trusting the answers. Accessing what you know is a process of relearning a new language, so it takes time. Often, people second-guess answers they receive and tell me that they "heard" an answer but didn't believe it. They actually block out the information, later realizing that the first answer was the true response. What's most important is to begin really asking and then really trusting. Put yourself in a program, almost like school, where you're learning something new. Expect to feel uncomfortable and uncertain, wondering if you're doing it "right."

There is no right or wrong, only practicing long enough to begin knowing yourself INSIDE so you can trust your own answers. Remember, you've been conditioned to go outside of yourself for information. You're learning a more natural rhythm of inner guidance.

Answers always come forth. You are the only obstacle to receiving them loud and clear. Once you commit to practicing in silence, you will be able to tap your own knowing in every situation. And eventually this will be the only voice you implicitly trust.

I used to think I knew myself pretty well. I worked in a creative field, relying on my intuition to produce television projects and work with creative people. My senses were tuned to what was not said in order to understand what to create. Unlike most businesses, there was total permission for the "off the wall," illogical ideas. Everyone knew that today's offbeat idea could be tomorrow's new trend. This intuitive environment provided a good foundation for understanding knowing.

The unexplained and illogical were not preposterous. In fact, that was where we'd start. For most people in today's left-brained, linear world, logic is the place to start. Therein lies the challenge. You have been conditioned to use logic to create your life. That is never the way your Soul talks to you.

The key point here is to give yourself permission to trust what you innately know. No matter how you know or sense something, it is as valid as scientifically proven knowledge. While this may sound wrong, it's not. When you are making decisions for yourself based on your own knowing, you are the barometer, not what someone else has to say.

A young man once came to me. He'd been working at a TV network for ten years as a researcher. He never really loved his job and *knew* that he'd rather be doing something else. Finally, at the ten-year mark, he began to question what he might do, even contemplating a change in work. But when I asked him how he would consider making a change, he indicated he had to be sure there was no risk. He had to feel certain he'd go to a secure job. The irony in his locked-in view of what he'd allow for himself is that on a deep level he knew this was the wrong work, yet on another level he blocked that information and convinced himself of what he should do. Nowhere in his framework for change was there trust that his own knowing ultimately could lead to what he really wanted: more satisfying work.

Without understanding the significance of having an internal divining rod—his knowing—he had forced himself into a life and had no way out. He'd never built any reliance on and trust in what he knew, deep inside.

Consider a different way to view his situation. A young man has known for ten years that he's drawn to something more fulfilling. He also knows he's terrified he'll fail if he makes the change. Yet, deep inside, he remembers that whenever he's followed his heart, everything worked out much better. Even if it was scarier than staying the course, he felt more alive, more satisfied, and more content. So he concludes that he can trust whatever guidance he is getting from within himself as he considers his options. In other words, he'll know when an opportunity feels right. Even if it looks too risky, he can trust this part of himself. Without relying on anyone else's opinions, he'll *know* what's best.

The fact is that your *knowing* happens all the time, whether you are aware of it or not. The question is whether you consciously use what you know or whether you dismiss it as illogical and unimportant.

Why would you discount information that comes so clearly and so easily? Why does what you know have to come from thinking and analyzing? Intuition focuses you on knowing. Why not benefit from a natural ability?

One of the best ways to lean into your own knowing is to trust your intuition. When your gut gives you guidance, listen to it. In fact, rather than analyze your decisions, use your gut first.

Ask yourself:

- How do I feel about this?
- What do I sense?
- What seems "off"?
- What nagging thought just won't go away?
- What feels right in my heart?

These kinds of questions lead you to develop, rather than override, the intuitive side of yourself. Trusting your intuitive ability leads you step-by-step to a deep appreciation for your own wisdom. This takes practice, but is so worth the result because eventually the more you trust your intuitive voice, from inside, the more you can tap your own deep knowing. It is that wisdom that lives in your heart and, with compassion, you discover the clarity of understanding.

Knowing from your heart is not painful or dramatic. In some ways, it is quite subtle. There is calmness and inner resolve that centers you in all decisions. Even when the mind interferes to add confusion or doubt, the heart always wins out. You cannot question the knowing of the heart. You literally stop listening outside of yourself; others' opinions no longer matter. In fact, you rarely ask for counsel. You just know the direction that is best for you. The peace and contentment that comes with knowing is what Everyday Soul is all about.

It is our birthright to live from our hearts. It is our job to develop the tools within ourselves to do just that. Just focus intuitively and you will automatically develop more inner knowing.

Remember that everything you need to know is already inside of you. You have an inner wisdom about everything.

You do not need to search for answers outside yourself. Look for that which on the outside resonates with you inside—that will lead you to the truth.

It's time to choose how you spend your time and energy. Go inside and explore.

Commit to the practice of asking and listening. Your intuition tunes you to hearing.

Your heart leads you to knowing.

CHECKPOINTS: *Where Are You Now?*

- How often do you sense something or "know" it and dismiss it?
- Think of a time when your intuition made a difference. Did you trust yourself then?
- Are you listening to others as you make decisions or yourself?
- Is there something now that you "know" needs to change?
- How can you use your intuition more?
- What's in the way of you believing that what you know matters?

Principles for Reflection

Work with these principles:

- *The ability to know is the most important innate talent you can ever develop.*

- *Knowing describes your innate inner sense of what is right for you, what fits and what does not.*

- *The depth of who you are lives inside the openness of your heart. When you live connected to your heart, what you feel, sense, and trust is centered in spirit. There is no need for outer noise, interference of others, or fear. Each step in life leads you to greater knowing from your heart.*

- *If you practice trusting information that comes from deep within you, you strengthen your ability to know all the time.*

- *To rekindle this innate inner knowing, you need silence and a commitment to listening.*

- *Tuning into the inner "vault" inside you is what allows you to "know." Your breath unlocks that knowing so you can begin to release all the outer interference.*

- *There is no right or wrong, only practicing long enough to begin knowing yourself INSIDE so you can trust your own answers. Remember, you've been conditioned to go outside of yourself for information. You're learning a more natural rhythm of inner guidance.*

- *Remember that everything you need to know is already inside of you. You have an inner wisdom about everything.*

CHAPTER FOUR

ℰXCELLENCE
Your Gift of Excellence

INSPIRATION
Life is either a daring adventure or nothing.

HELEN KELLER

A connection to your Soul requires that you see yourself differently. No longer imperfect, flawed, or bad, you must recognize your natural areas of excellence, the abilities that are inherently easy for you. These are the things at which, with very little effort, you naturally excel. Your understanding of these talents and what makes them uniquely yours represents a link to your happiness. And it requires a new respect for the mystery of who you are upon birth.

No one else gives you this excellence. There is no school where you learn what you're good at, you just innately have the talent. When someone has incredible innate talent, that person is often described as a "child prodigy," a special child gifted with exceptional talent. While that may be accurate, the fact is that we are all child prodigies in our own way. We are all gifted with exceptional talents. This is how the universe works. Reflect for a moment on this. Is a sunflower more exceptional than a rose? Is an evergreen tree more exceptional than a willow? Is a blue jay more exceptional than a loon? Of course not. The same goes for people, too.

> *We each have certain gifts that are ours to bring into the world. Some people may describe this as "God-given" which may be accurate, but regardless of how the blessings came to be, the fact is that you have an excellence that is yours at birth. You can build a life around your natural excellence.*

Some people understand this immediately and begin to create a life around their natural gifts or talents, while others miss this important understanding. The reason most of us miss this truth is because we live in a world that tells us that we know nothing of value at birth. We must learn what we need to know. Our orientation is that a baby is helpless and dependent, and while he or she has an aptitude to learn, he or she inherently knows very little that is useful. This is so far from the truth that it's no wonder so many people live large parts of their lives without connecting to their Souls.

Imagine if your parents had been educated to believe that you had gifts to bring to the world, right from the start. That you actually had wisdom of your own to share and it was their job to uncover that knowledge and assist you in bringing it into the world. Not exert their own wishes on you, not mold you into their way, and not discard what you innately do well. Just imagine how differently you may have walked each step of your life. Unfortunately, the idea of an infinitely wise child from birth is relatively new, so most of us have not been guided through childhood with the support to nurture whatever comes *naturally*. Instead, we are conditioned to believe we must work hard to overcome our weaknesses. To excel means working hard to be better than we already are, better than we *naturally are*.

The work of the Soul is exactly the opposite. There are NO weaknesses, only opportunities for growth. The only focus is to uncover your strengths and nourish them. And, most important, to stretch your potential to limits *beyond* your reach, all the while *trusting* the inspiration that arises from focusing on your natural abilities. Your weaknesses will be healed as you generate healthy respect for your gifts.

This orientation is key to living a life of Everyday Soul because you know that what you *are* good at is where you excel. And your real job in life is to find that innate talent, nourish it, and bring it to the world fully. There is no right or wrong way to do this because you trust that your purpose here is to bring these gifts out.

If you only focused on who you are with respect to this excellence, imagine how much less you would suffer. No more comparisons to others, no more wondering if you're on the right track, or following what you think you should do. You would fully believe in yourself and why you're walking on the planet.

Understanding natural excellence is important because this treasure chest of innate gifts links directly to your Soul.

The Ease of Excellence

One of my clients usually started his sessions apologizing for what he hadn't yet accomplished, based on plans from the previous session. He obviously felt inadequate and guilty. Conditioned by years of disapproval from teachers and parents, he found my response refreshing. I always said, "That's fine, you just weren't ready to do that yet. When you are, you will." In other words, I trusted that his innate abilities were guiding him as to what was next, step-by-step. If he had also trusted himself, he would have known that when he easily accomplished whatever he'd wanted to do, it would have been done in sync with his own energy. Instead, he was weighed down by the sense that he wasn't doing enough or not doing it right, leading him to feel "wrong" a great deal of the time.

Linking to his Soul every day was a challenge because he didn't even trust his own inner guidance on simple activities, which made it difficult for him to believe he had innate talent—something good enough within him that could guide him toward whatever was right to do. This disconnect from inner talents occurs in all of us. The irony is that excellence comes naturally to all of us, not in all things, but in very important ways.

Think of what you do easily, what requires little effort, and what you are rewarded for over and over again. This is your natural excellence.

Often people even comment on how good you are at whatever it is you do. You even stop thinking about how you do whatever it is, because it's so natural, it's just "who you are."

We've all heard people describe others using phrases like "She's a social butterfly and can talk to anyone," or "He can figure out the answer to any problem," or "She has a way with words." These are clues to natural excellence: traits that others see come naturally to you. If you follow your history, you can track these innate abilities recurring time and time again in your life. You are drawn into situations that use your talents. The sad part is that you *could consciously* build a life around your gifts, yet do not. Rather than a life of satisfaction doing what is naturally fulfilling to you, you end up with the bulk of activities in your life keeping you busy but not contented. An assortment of experiences is not really a meaningful life.

> *If you understand your natural talents, you can shape a life around them, and your sense of fulfillment will be immense.*

Another client I coach told me that ever since he was a kid he's been fascinated with sports—"obsessed" his mother called it. He remembered every statistic, read anything he could get his hands on, and followed the details of all sports events. He had even considered a career in sports, but sometime around high school his family discouraged him, telling him it wouldn't be possible. So in college, he majored in business and forged a career in the banking industry. Years and years later, turning sports into his weekend fun, he felt stifled by banking and empty. His only joy now came on the weekends.

In contrast, a good friend has a fourteen-year-old daughter who has always been a free spirit of sorts. My friend's orientation to mothering has been to foster whatever natural aptitude her kids exhibit and encourage them to explore their interests fully, allowing room for any option to develop. Here's an example of how she did this. When her daughter was six, they lived in New York City. Exiting the apartment building each day, her daughter would immediately let go of her hand and furiously race ahead of her mother, running and exploring. This panicked my friend, of course, but once she got her daughter safely in tow, rather than scold her and contain her, my friend realized that her daughter's exploring nature was who she was *innately*. She needed to be able to move freely and see what was of interest. This was not a rebellious reaction; this was who she really was. So they moved to a very rural area where the cherished days when children safely roam the town were still possible. This little girl thrived in a setting that supported her, rather than being stifled and forced to change.

Now, as a teenager, she sees something of interest and tells her mother she'd like to know more about it. Recently, as they were driving, she saw a sign for Save the Children. Her daughter's first reaction was to ask to go see what they do in that place. In other words, her innate nature has been nurtured and remains intact so she, herself, trusts it enough to act on it. She's been given permission to be herself. Out of being herself will come an excellence unique to her.

Search for Your Excellence

When you're looking for clues to your own natural excellence or what's innately your ability or interest, go back to childhood. Remember what you were most attracted to, search for what people said about you, and uncover whatever you threw away as impossible.

At age five, I can remember praying every night for all the animals hurt or lost or killed by accident. We were not a religious family at all, but I had picked up that prayer was important, so every night, faithfully, I asked for God to help the animals. A bit later, I began to read all the dog books I could find. I studied every breed. Just like the sports nut, I was a dog nut. Somewhere in high school, that took a backseat. And eventually, the only trace left was an overwhelming urge as an adult to help the animals. But my professional life steered me so far from animals it wasn't funny. Secretly, I vowed I would someday help animals. Today, I sit on a 183-acre farm, a sanctuary for Border collies in need of rescue. About 150 dogs find safety at our farm each year. I am excelling at what I do. It's so natural for me to be working with dogs, and yet it took so long to find this joy. It's hard to believe it took forty-six years to finally land here, following what was *innately so loud as a child*. Yet no one nurtured it, no one guided me toward it. Luckily, with enough personal growth, I still found my way. That's why I help others do the same. I hear this from people *all the time*.

The clues to your happiness are loudly present in childhood.

One way to see what you believe about yourself is to honestly answer these questions:

- Did you give up something you loved to do for work in favor of something you "should" do?
- Are you dissatisfied when the results of your efforts aren't perfect?
- Do you easily accept compliments for what you do?
- Do you feel stifled by the lack of options in your life now?
- Has there been something you've always wanted to do and didn't?
- If money were no object, what would you be doing?

Natural excellence comes so easily that you often overlook the importance or value of what you can do. It seems unimportant if it comes without effort. You are conditioned to believe this to be true. It is not.

I ask every client I work with some simple questions: What do you do that is effortless? What is so easy that you don't even remember learning how to do it? Their answers always reveal where the joy lies, where the connection to the Soul can be found.

The way you find fulfillment in living is by using your innate talents. Your purpose in life is to bring these gifts out, not keep them bottled up, wishing someday to express them.

The longing within you to manifest these abilities is immense and grows louder and louder until, finally, a life review is necessary. You are the only one able to acknowledge this deep desire and take steps to express it in life. The key is remembering why you are here. You need courage to take the step to make changes in your life. The payoff is how your heart feels. Your heart is aligned, inside and out.

When you bring your natural excellence into the world, the world rewards you.

You will receive acknowledgment for what you contribute. That is how the Soul works. But you will be required to let go of fantasies about how this looks. Whatever you can imagine is far smaller than what is possible when you let your Soul guide you. You must let go.

Examples of natural excellence are easy to see in nature: the beautiful shine of a peacock's green and blue feathers; the fiery orange glow of a fading sun streaking through the sky; the unique crystals of snow and ice where no one form is ever repeated. These illustrate a bigger story of grand perfection. We are part of this creativity, so why wouldn't we, too, have unique gifts to express? Wouldn't we naturally come into the world with our own excellence?

A young woman I coach is a teacher who works with college-age adults. When she discusses her accomplishments, she beams with pride. It is not an egotistical pride, it is a joy-filled sense of feeling that she has helped others. In turn, the kids have written her numerous letters of gratitude for the example she set with her style of teaching. She guides them toward confidence in their abilities, nurtures them through confusion, and always offers her own example of humanity, imperfect as it is. She quickly conveys a strong sense of belonging. She is right where she needs to be. There is deep fulfillment in her work, and she excels at what she does. The students feel her stability because it's coming from deep within her. She naturally excels as a teacher and as an inspiration for others.

When you utilize your innate talents, there is peace in what is done. This client feels it every day she works with her students. She does not doubt herself.

In contrast, in another area of her life, her innate talents are not as evident. She mistrusts her ability to mother a child because she has no model for good mothering. She feels inadequate, insecure, and uncertain that she will succeed. In essence, she cannot find any natural talent that seems instinctive. When she thinks of parenting, she is fearful, and feels awkward and very uneasy. A completely different person emerges, right before your eyes.

This example is a good snapshot of the difference between innate talents and learned talents. What's easy is innate and brings great satisfaction. What is not is a struggle, generating a sense of unworthiness, doubt, and fear. In her case, she will have to relearn mothering as an adult, teaching herself what a good mother can be. This will require effort and patience, since it will not come naturally. Every step will put her out of balance, until she actually finds the places within the experience of mothering where she *does* excel. Something will emerge as natural for her. Whether it be nurturing the child, communicating with the child, or introducing the child to new experiences— some aspect of mothering will be created uniquely in her own approach. Not her mother's approach or some textbook style, but with her innate ability she will develop her own excellence in this area, too.

> *If you shift your belief to an appreciation for all that is*
> *excellent in the world, you will quickly include yourself.*
> *Living each day with a focus on bringing that intuitive*
> *competence out of hiding will reshape the life you lead.*
> *All that is required is your courage to do so.*

Client after client comes to me for coaching, and almost all of them follow the same pattern: They have all experienced the joy of being effortlessly good at something, truly excellent, and yet almost all of them block out the very activity that could bring them joy. Somewhere in their lives they've believed that designing a life around something so easy cannot be done. They actually walk away from the very thing that gives them joy. They choose a harder route, working at an activity that requires a push to accomplish and creates continual pressure on them. It's as if they feel more comfortable "not being good enough" at what they do, rather than being excellent at what they do.

Think about this in relation to yourself and others you know. We don't have a frame of reference for natural excellence except in athletes, musicians, and those "extraordinary" people who seem gifted. So-called "regular people" have no model for excellence. The pervasive model that exists is one of dedication and hard work, persevering beyond all obstacles, continually pushing to succeed. The picture of an uphill battle is the norm for most people. Professional work is work, not play. It is not considered appropriate for work to be a joy. This is why I see so many clients dissatisfied with their lives. On a very deep level, they compromised what brings them joy in the name of some rule of adulthood. The prevailing attitude is that only the "exceptional people" can live outside the rules.

Of course, this is not true. Your Soul has no frame of reference for rules. The exceptional is the norm. Look around. Using nature as a guide, what is an example of excellence? Can you judge what one thing is better than another? What gives a bumblebee the right to more joy than a trout? What gives an ant more freedom to be itself than a hawk? These questions point out the ludicrous way in which we humans box ourselves in.

Finding your natural excellence means getting out of the box and owning the gifts you can bring to the world.

Review your life, your work, your love—and let yourself accept the truth about what you do well. Then go deeper. Uncover what you do so naturally that it is excellent. Choose to support that part of yourself with all your time, energy, and passion. Be willing to let go of the results, the fantasies, and the beliefs that limit what's possible. And cherish the satisfaction that comes once you contribute to the world from your Soul.

Excellence brings deep contentment to the heart.

CHECKPOINTS: *Where Are You Now?*

- Do you believe you have strong skills that are unique to you?
- Are there times when you feel that none of your talents are very special?
- What have you been noticed for over and over again?
- What stands in the way of your shaping a life around those talents?
- Is there anything you've always felt you were particularly good at but cannot do or have not done professionally?
- Based on what you know about your talents, what would be a truly satisfying work experience?

Principles for Reflection

Work with these principles:

- *We each have certain gifts that are ours to bring into the world. Some people may describe this as "God-given," which may be accurate, but regardless of how the blessings came to be, the fact is that you have an excellence that is yours at birth. You can build a life around your natural excellence.*

- *Understanding natural excellence is important because this treasure chest of innate gifts links directly to your Soul.*

- *If you understand your natural talents, you can shape a life around them, and your sense of fulfillment will be immense.*

- *When you're looking for clues to your own natural excellence or what's innately your ability or interest, go back to childhood. Remember what you were most attracted to, search for what people said about you, and uncover whatever you threw away as impossible.*

- *The way you find fulfillment in living is by using your innate talents. Your purpose in life is to bring these gifts out, not keep them bottled up, wishing someday to express them.*

- *When you bring your natural excellence into the world, the world rewards you.*

- *If you shift your belief to an appreciation for all that is excellent in the world, you will quickly include yourself. Living each day with a focus on bringing that intuitive competence out of hiding will reshape the life you lead. All that is required is your courage to do so.*

CHAPTER FIVE

ABUNDANCE
Plenty for You

INSPIRATION
Be realistic: Plan for a miracle

BHAGWA RAJNEESH

Have you ever heard good news about a friend and somewhere inside felt a bit jealous, thinking, "Why can't that happen to me?" If you're honest, the answer is yes. When someone else receives something good, we naturally feel there is less for us. We've been conditioned to believe this, not because it's true but because the world appears to us to have limited resources. That's how the business world operates. Whoever has the most of an item in demand gets the most money because eventually there won't be any more. We often translate that to our personal lives, thinking if something is scarce, there won't be enough for us.

There are just so many jobs available and once they are filled, there are no more. The message is clear: Get yours while you can because tomorrow it may be gone. We reference examples of limited resources when we construct our lives.

We rarely take into account the examples of abundance.

Abundance literally means "a great or plentiful amount," "fullness to overflowing."

Think for a moment of some examples of abundance:

The galaxy with billions of stars
Rays of sunshine reaching around the world
Millions of insects covering the earth
Snowflakes in a blizzard
The number of cars Detroit manufactures each year
The number of supermarkets stocked full of food in every city in the United States
Every home with running water
Every letter mailed each day
The billions of people alive today

We actually witness abundance all around us, yet scarcity is our call to action. It's what motivates us to compete, to excel, to lie, to steal, to cheat, to worry, and to doubt. No matter how much of any one thing is around us, all we see is what isn't there.

From what you know about your Soul and living in connection to this treasure within you, what frame of reference makes sense? The one with limited perspective, or the one with infinite potential for creation?

Choosing abundance is exactly that: a choice. You are in charge of what influences your judgment. If you allow scarcity to be your framework, that is all you will ever see, but if you foster abundance as your vision, the anxiety of "missing out" will dissipate and a calm contentment will grow.

A wise teacher once said to me, "All the resources you need will be there when you need them." I struggled with that concept because, in fact, I had not consciously seen it in action. It seemed more accurate to say, "I have to fight for everything I need." But rather than dismiss this wisdom, I chose to embrace it and literally put it into practice every time anxiety prevailed. I worked with this teaching in all aspects of living. I said, "I'll arrive at the time that is right" rather than worrying that I was going to be late. "The right person will be there to help me" rather than dreading who I'd encounter. "What's happening at any given time is for my highest good" rather than thinking, "Oh, here we go again."

What occurred as a result was miraculous. Living in an abundant state didn't mean I suddenly had all the money I wanted, no troubles whatsoever, and peace and serenity. What actually happened was far simpler. I felt relieved to get rid of the worry, fear, and doubt. I *trusted* that there was plenty for me and for everyone.

My own sense of existing with others no longer carried a "them or me" undercurrent. And my shift changed their interactions with me. The struggle between people reacting to scarce resources stopped happening. I experienced trust within myself for receiving whatever was needed. I connected to my Soul and the more spiritual side of me, rather than the purely human side. I finally felt what the Soul knows. There is eternity. Infinity is real. We distrust this because we forget on a very, very deep level what we know:

We are held by something far greater than ourselves. There is an infinite wisdom in the universe and we are part of it.

Borrowing on the experience of nature, imagine yourself as a rock in the Grand Canyon, existing for millions upon millions of years, witnessing evolutionary change on a grandiose scale. If you were that rock (I know it's hard to imagine, but just try), would you anticipate that each occurrence signaled your demise? That other rocks were working against you? That you were the only rock suffering this lonely, difficult life stuck in the bottom of the largest canyon in the world? Why, oh why couldn't you be as big as you once were, before the Ice Age? This may seem absurd, but from your Soul's point of view, petty worries like these are just as ridiculous.

> *The viewpoint from which you judge yourself is so limited and myopic that you are missing the most important understanding of abundance: You are part of something far larger than just you. Harmony and chaos work in tandem to create your growth, which you call your life. You are evolving just as everything else around you evolves. An abundant orientation expands, rather than restricts, what is possible.*

A professional client I coach was in the middle of changing jobs, in search of an executive-level position. The marketplace was tight with seemingly few options due to a slumping economy. She had been working on her personal growth for the last three years, so rather than let the facts defeat her, she was able to maintain an attitude of abundance, approaching her search in a totally different way. She did not subscribe to the idea that "it would be tough," that "the marketplace was saturated with people at her level," that "it would take a long time." Instead, she oriented her beliefs this way: The right opportunity would become available when the timing was right for her; what she had to offer was unique and valuable to the right employer; and it would go smoothly with unexpected surprises to consider. Rather than worry about a limited selection, over six months' time, she calmly and clearly found a better job that met her goals. Remember that an abundant perspective is full of possibilities, unlimited options yet to be revealed. There is no scarcity. Holding this belief creates a different result.

Another client once called me in tears, worried about the decisions she faced. Her twelve-year-old, million-dollar construction business was falling apart and losing significant revenue, her husband had left her, and a divorce was imminent. She had created a new business venture with enough investment backing to launch it, but she felt confused about what to do.

Coaching her from an abundant orientation, I questioned if she'd always wanted to own the construction business—was it a forever desire? She said no, in fact; she'd felt stifled recently, less interested and itching for something new. I asked her if she'd always wanted to be married forever. She said yes, but she'd always doubted her decision to marry her husband. While so much had worked well, so much had been out of sync. In her gut, she'd had her doubts. I asked her to review her life and notice how varied her experiences had been. From a long-term perspective, she realized that over the years she'd always had a lot of changes, new things, new people, and new opportunities, and whenever she felt somewhat bored, she'd end up in something new. Once she realized that her approach had always opened up options for her rather than restricted them, she was able to put the current changes in perspective. The loss of the construction company didn't mean the end for her; it meant another opportunity was developing. In fact, she already had this well underway. The loss of her husband didn't mean the end for her, either; it meant she was ready for a more appropriate partner. From an understanding of the abundance available in the universe, she was just growing in a new direction and re-creating her life, yet again. She could then reframe this "tragic" time with new understanding.

Again, to borrow on an example from nature, if there are billions and billions of stars in the galaxy showing us the principle of abundance, how could there only be one job for each one us? One person for each of us? Wouldn't there be many, many options that could fit us? The more you connect to your Soul, the more you realize that you are never limited in any aspect of your life. It's you who creates a belief system that supports scarcity. It's you who can change that.

The Choice Is Yours

Choosing an abundant orientation as a way of being in your life is up to you. There isn't much around you to support this choice because most of the world isn't that evolved yet. You will need courage to hold to a view that will cause most people to laugh. Remember, in many ways we are still in the Dark Ages. We may think we're the most advanced, intelligent species at the moment, but we are not. Just like the boulder changed by the Ice Age into a small rock, we are merely works in progress.

> *Your job is to hold the highest understanding that relates to your Soul, not the lowest perspective as in "an eye for an eye." You will feel the difference when you live with abundance as your belief.*

One area where clients always have the most trouble with abundance is money. No matter how open they are to accepting a new perspective, they still only see what is in their bank account as reality. Yet when I point out the number of millionaires in the United States alone, they have to admit that plenty of money does exist. They also agree that the majority of millionaires are self-made people, which again is an example of infinite potential, not restriction. The difference between the millionaires and them is that those who earn those millions actually believed it was possible to receive that level of earning. They reconditioned their beliefs to allow themselves great monetary abundance. Rather than see others having it and feeling they never could, they decided they would. In other words, all the money was there; they just had to shape their beliefs that *they* could have it.

An interesting fact that illustrates the difficulties we have accepting abundance as a concept comes from a truth about lottery winners. Almost all of the people who win millions of dollars—enough to cover their needs for a lifetime—will lose the money within one year of receiving it. An odd fact, but if you understand the belief of scarcity, then you'll understand why even when they have all that money, they cannot keep it. They do not believe abundance is possible.

What You Believe Matters

Your beliefs create your life. Everything around you that you experience comes from your beliefs. Everything.

The lottery winners spent most of their lives believing they would never have enough money. They came from an orientation of scarcity—"if only one day." So when they won, they had to exhaust the money to return to the feeling of not having enough—the feeling they were used to and comfortable with. Their entire life was structured around not having money rather than having it. In contrast, a child born into a very wealthy family knows with certainty that money will never be a concern. His or her belief structure supports abundance, so the issue of scarcity never comes up.

Which experience is accurate in life? Is there not enough money to go around? Or is there plenty of money? The answer differs according to your belief.

Another good example is Bill Cosby. From the inner city of New York, his childhood was tough and his destiny looked far from ideal. In fact, the statistics supported his failure, not success. Scarcity was a way of life in Harlem. Grim examples of horrible lives surrounded him, yet on some deep level, he held a belief that he could have more. Step-by-step, he kept that belief alive and changed his entire life forever.

So what is reality? It's important to ask how you formed the answer to this question.

Learning to believe that abundance is possible will be a process. You've been conditioned over many, many years to doubt that you deserve to receive anything easily. The American attitude is also contradictory. The country rests on the foundation that there is enough for everyone, but in practice, the overriding principle is more about survival of the fittest.

So you will doubt that abundance is possible. You will distrust yourself for being unrealistic. You will dismiss the sensation of your Soul when you finally feel at ease because it actually feels more normal to be competing with others. Remember, it actually feels more *normal* to be competing with others.

Think about this. Do you realize how powerful this conditioning is in your life?

The overriding cultural teaching is to "be good to others, but make sure to get what is yours." You've been taught that there isn't enough for everyone.

What you're attempting to do is erase the brainwashed definition of "normal" and create your own belief of what is possible and real. You must have courage to step away from the group ideas and forge your own understanding. This courage is nourished when you link to your Soul.

Developing a spiritual life that reinforces principles of abundance is the only way to really shift your beliefs.

What you're doing is somewhat similar to what the Wright brothers did in believing flight was possible. Ostracized and mocked, they held steady to their vision, never dismayed by outside opinions, and, of course, their beliefs led to the invention of the airplane.

You have to decide to believe in abundance, find others to support you, and then hold steady to experience abundance in action. It may take repeated attempts, over years, before you actually shift your belief, but it will happen if you persist.

As you view scarcity versus abundance, listen carefully to those around you. You are tuning in to their beliefs as you hear them speak about everyday situations:

"I waited and waited to hear from that guy, but he never called me back. It figures." Versus an abundant thinker: I never heard from that guy, which is just as well because a better-suited person will now emerge and it will be easier.

"We have no more money left to pay the bills." Versus an abundant thinker: I trust the money will come to me in some unexpected way to pay the bills just in time. *Or:* I guess I'll have a new way to earn that money soon.

"Everyone I know is having babies. I'm going to be too old if I don't have a baby soon." Versus *an abundant thinker:* I'll be pregnant when the timing is right for me, and I trust that a greater force is at work to make it happen, if it's right.

Honoring the Mystery

Abundant thinkers see possibilities, endless possibilities. There is always an open door, an option beyond the facts.

Why would that be reasonable to assume? Just look at the mystery of creation. Could we, with all our knowledge, actually create every variety of leaf that exists on the trees on this planet? Can we, with all our facts, create a thunderstorm that moves across the entire globe? Are we, with complete certainty, able to explain why the body can heal itself? In other words, there is mystery in life.

Abundant thinkers acknowledge the mystery and invite this infinite wisdom to assist. They expect unusual occurrences.

They welcome upheaval and absurdity because they know it's the sign of re-creation. A greater hand is at work re-creating the situation far beyond what they can imagine as humans seeing the small view of life they see.

An abundant vision is one that accounts for the fact that there is no way for you to see and know everything. You can never know the whole picture of reality. It's impossible.

So, rather than subscribe to the philosophy of scarcity, really recognize the overriding principle at work all around you—abundance.

Abundance is a spiritual principle at work on our planet. There are countless examples of it around us. When you delve into the real facts behind situations that appear to represent scarcity, human hands are usually to blame. Humans have made the decisions that cause the problems. Even people fighting to feed the hungry all over the world state the fact that there is more than enough food for everyone. Issues of allocation cause scarcity.

The human experience is to thrive on competition because we have not yet evolved into caring for all; we are still self-focused. Our personal agendas matter more than the need to care for all people. Do you now see why abundant thinking isn't the norm?

Test yourself for a moment. Try focusing on your heart and the love you have for others you know.

- Is there a scarcity of your love for them?
- Is it possible to run out of love?
- Where does that love come from so that you don't run out?
- How can you love so many people, animals, and experiences equally?

Now pick something you have always viewed in one way—your job or your personal situation will do. Challenge yourself to explore the various options that actually exist. . . . What other ways could this look? In what other ways could this be done? Are you seeing this from a perspective of scarcity or abundance? Do you believe you have other options?

If you can begin to believe that whatever you need will be there for you, then you can change your view of everything around you.

CHECKPOINTS: *Where Are You Now?*

- How do you form what you believe about abundance versus scarcity?
- What's your first reaction to bad news? To good news?
- Do you believe you can have everything you want? If so, why? If not, why not?
- What's an example of abundance in your life now?

- What did you see that made you feel that "there isn't enough to go around"?
- Can you trust that what is yours will come to you?

Principles for Reflection

Work with these principles:

- *Abundance literally means "a great or plentiful amount," "fullness to overflowing."*

- *Choosing abundance is exactly that: a choice. You are in charge of what influences your judgment. If you allow scarcity to be your framework, that is all you will ever see, but if you foster abundance as your vision, the anxiety of "missing out" will dissipate and a calm contentment will grow.*

- *The viewpoint from which you judge yourself is so limited and myopic that you are missing the most important understanding of abundance: You are part of something far larger than just you. Harmony and chaos work in tandem to create your growth, which you call your life. You are evolving just as everything else around you evolves. An abundant orientation expands, rather than restricts, what is possible.*

- *Your job is to hold the highest understanding that relates to your Soul, not the lowest perspective as in "an eye for an eye." You will feel the difference when you live with abundance as your belief.*

- *Your beliefs create your life. Everything around you that you experience comes from your beliefs. Everything.*

- *Abundant thinkers see possibilities, endless possibilities. There is always an open door, an option beyond the facts.*

- *Abundant thinkers acknowledge the mystery and invite this infinite wisdom to assist. They expect unusual occurrences.*

- *An abundant vision is one that accounts for the fact that there is no way for you to see and know everything. You can never know the whole picture of reality. It's impossible.*

CHAPTER SIX

PRESENT MOMENT
Being Here Now

INSPIRATION
*It is impossible to care for the Soul
and live at the same time in unconsciousness.*

THOMAS MOORE

The Soul is a creative guiding force that comes only from the present, not the past or the future. Linking to that life force requires that you learn how to disconnect from the past and let go of worries about the future.

The present moment is the most fundamental key to unlocking your connection to your Soul. The energy you feel from living in the present is nourishing, healing, and regenerative.

A simple illustration of present moment comes from the dogs surrounding me at the farm. They rise each day with an incredible amount of energy, ready for excitement and adventure. There is no overhang from the day before. They are completely thrilled to see me, wildly jumping around, kissing me, demanding and giving affection. Their greeting is the best reminder of how we should live, so happy and alive at the start of another day. Any animal living with you can teach you about present moment because this is what animals do so well. They don't worry about their bills, schedules, and plans—or their mistakes and regrets. They literally show up each day aware that they are here. They show us what being *in the present* is all about.

The same is true for children, which is why they, too, have unbounded energy. Haven't you ever wondered why *you* have less energy? We think it's all about age, but that's not the whole truth. Why would their innocence give them more energy? We tend to think it's because they have no worries. But, again, that's only half the truth. It's really about the present moment. They don't yet know, and dogs never will know, the need for the past or future. Their reality happens in the present. Just imagine how light and free and alive you'd feel if you, too, could release your history and your worries about tomorrow. You would be freed up to be here now; nothing else would matter.

To better understand why present moment matters, think for a moment about your energy.

You are a life force of energy that you focus in various ways each moment. When you are focused on the past, that energy is not available in the current moment. You have engaged it elsewhere. And the same is true when you focus on the future.

All great artists, writers, scientists, and athletes will tell you that there are moments when they are so focused on the task at hand that they have no sense of time at all. Many people have usually experienced this in some way, maybe in sports or childbirth or a celebration, or when in love. The event or task at hand is so consuming that all of your energy is present. Your energy is not split in various directions.

For most people, the sensation of being in the present is very, very fulfilling. You feel more connected, more alive, and more aware of everything that matters. This is possible *every day* if you know how to refocus from the past and future to the present, consciously. You actually learn how to shift your energy from one orientation to another, thereby allowing you to be more creative, more energetic, and more satisfied.

Think of your energy like a bank. You have lots of energy saved. You withdraw what you need for various activities. If you have a big event from the past or a trauma that still bothers you, then that withdrawal is still gone. If you have doubts and concerns about a future need, then you withdraw energy for that, too. Again, it's gone from your overall account. Now add up all the things on your list for which you are withdrawing energy, related to the past or future. Can you see why you're so tired in the present? Why you feel defeated now, before you even take action? Your energy bank account is already depleted.

Where Is Your Energy?

Easterners describe westerners as having "monkey mind." This is an attempt to illustrate how our minds jump from thing to thing, like a monkey from tree to tree. We are unable to focus. If you've ever attempted a quiet meditation, you can see how the monkey mind concept is accurate. Just when you are still and calm, your mind will throw in an idea, leading you to think about something. Then, moments later, another idea. Then, another and another and another. We have not been trained to manage our energy and focus. It's no wonder we are tired. We are literally sending our energy all over time and space.

When you want to tune in and hear your Soul's guidance,
it's very hard to do if you are everywhere but in the moment.

Usually the clutter in the mind is so consuming that we rarely give anything attention for very long. Almost everyone can remember sitting with a friend, telling a story, and feeling that the person wasn't even at the table, wasn't even listening. When you are focused in the past or future, it's as if you are physically present but not emotionally, mentally, or spiritually present. The other person can feel this and so can you, once you learn the difference between being "present" and being in some other frame of mind. You notice an empty feeling, like no one is paying attention. This is how your Soul experiences you when you are not in the present moment. Your Soul is always trying to guide you, and yet no one is home, no one is receiving.

The morning of September 11, 2001, was an amazing lesson in present moment awareness. Standing in front of the television, witnessing a moment-by-moment disaster live was what being in the present is all about. All other time was suspended. Each of us was forced to focus in a singular way on the news. Shortly thereafter, we began splitting our attention to caring for others. But at the moment the event unfolded, we were consumed. That is how it is for children and dogs—and anyone else lucky enough to know how to consciously move into the present. The experience is very rich, whether good or bad; it is saturated.

The startling contrast for me came once I stepped out of the house, after seeing what happened on 9/11. Here we had just felt sorrow and shock worse than anything before, yet outside our door the air was clean and fresh, the bees and birds sang as usual, and the dogs happily ran toward us for their normal attention. Life, to the thirty dogs on our farm, was absolutely no different. They were just as excited about today as they were about yesterday and as they would be about tomorrow. Some may say, "Well, they are just dogs." I say that what they know about living is worth studying. We can garner a meaningful understanding of life that brings us more joy, which is the Soul's work.

Unlocking the Present

Your past is not who you are today.

This fact is startlingly profound. If you can truly embrace this truth, then you can be free to manage all questions in your life. You can see yourself with fresh eyes, making much clearer decisions. Instead, most people feel obligated to their history, linked by some "rule" that says it matters.

Your past only matters if it's helping you become who you want to be today.

If you're allowing past history to weigh you down or hinder your actions, then you are stopping your own growth.

The present moment is all about growth. If you show up, with all your energy for everything in life, then you will be nourished and satisfied.

If you stifle yourself, for whatever obligation you assume, then your energy is blocked and your discontentment builds.

Most clients start working with me and discover that they are thoroughly involved in their past. They reference who they are now based on their past achievements and mark the sum total of experiences as if that is a way of knowing who they are now. Their homes are filled with pictures of memorable events, people, and occasions, even from their childhood. They still talk about previous activities as if they are happening now, though it's years later. One man continually tells the stories from his college years, though he is well into his sixties. He's not reminiscing—he actually still believes he is that person from that time. Of course, he is not. He's nowhere as vibrant, brave, or physically capable. But because that time carries the "best" energy for him, he still keeps his energy focused back then.

Another woman came to me for guidance in having a baby. In her late thirties, she had been to numerous fertility specialists, all unsuccessful. When she sat with me, she cried about her doubts that she could have a child. Past results certainly deemed her infertile. The first course of action was to bring back the energy of joy into her realm of experience. She needed to feel freedom from what surrounded her. As we worked quietly in meditation, breathing and visioning the new life possible inside of her, she began to cry. She shared her history with her mother: She'd never felt wanted and was left to mother herself. She shared her fears that she could ever be a good mother, considering her experiences. My job was clear. We had to release the past, which was preventing her from conceiving. A four-hour session of energy work and intuitive healing returned the sense of hope. We worked diligently to return her energy to the present and focus her on who she was today and what was possible now, after releasing the past burdens. Months later, she returned to the specialists and is now proudly carrying twins.

This woman's story is a classic example of how past energy impacts the future and your ability to be in the present. She was literally trapped by history. When she looked into the future, she was trapped by hopelessness. So when she attempted to use her energy to create a life, there was nothing present.

Your Energy Returns

The present moment is a place of creation. Your energetic force is powerful when you are aligned. You can feel the difference. If you're feeling stressed, overwhelmed, disheartened, agitated, or worried, you are not in the present.

In a recent workshop, I asked participants to write down their greatest fear in life, personal or professional. I invite you to do the same. Then, once it's written, ask yourself if this fear is based on the past, future, or present. In the workshop, every single person wrote down a fear based in the past or future. When I asked if they had this fear in the present, none did. In other words, the energetic disturbance they were creating had to do with something that had either already happened, something they feared would happen again, or something they feared would never happen. In the present, they had no energy left to create what they wanted.

A man had been working with me to change his profession after ten years. He had successfully attracted a new opportunity and was negotiating final terms. In each session he began to dwell on what was likely to come from the new venture. He was anticipating every move. While that may have been good for negotiations, it was not good for his energy. He was worrying, losing sleep, and was unsettled and irritable. When we began refocusing away from the future result and into what was literally right in front of his face, he calmed down and felt a sense of renewed strength. He was depleting his energy bank account by going into the future. He had to learn to stay in the moment, fully aware and responsive. From that place, he was able to create the future, step-by-step.

Living a life of Everyday Soul means becoming aware of where your energy is going so that you can effectively tune into present situations with your full life force.

When some idea unrelated to what you are currently doing comes into your head, practice casting it out. You will attend to the thoughts, but the goal is to live now and become accustomed to focusing in the present. What is important now? What requires your attention now? By catching yourself with these questions, you will have more energy to handle any situation.

The present moment is a very simple concept, yet a very challenging practice. Numerous books have been written teaching the value of this concept because it's one so often overlooked, yet it is so very important. To illustrate how little time you spend in the present moment, ask yourself:

- How many times while reading this have you thought of other things?
- How often has your "monkey mind" been at work?

Most people have a difficult time focusing on what is happening in the present. Instead, their mind takes them to other times and thoughts. Hasn't this been happening to you while reading? Trust me when I say that it's not the book causing you to go elsewhere mentally, it's your inexperience at knowing how to focus in the moment. A skilled athlete will tell you that the greatest challenge is keeping the mind on the moment at hand, rather than remembering past mistakes or anticipating what's to come.

We are very unskilled at being in the present moment. This will require a new focus, one you will need to develop.

If you truly want to challenge yourself, try this. Set the beeper on your watch to sound every fifteen minutes. At the moment it beeps, check where you went for the last fifteen minutes.

How many times did you jump back in time? How many times did you jump forward? The result of this exercise is twofold. You will be amazed at how often you are NOT present, and you can begin to practice being present. Think of this as your Present Moment Olympics. After checking in at fifteen-minute intervals, you will get better and better at staying present, not floating off to the past or future.

One of the easiest ways to bring yourself into the present moment is with your breathing. Breathe deeply a few times. You then become very aware of the life force that constantly feeds your body. Your body relaxes, and you move from out of your head into your body. You let go of emotions, move into your body, and begin to open your heart.

This is known as alignment: mind, body, soul. Most of your day is spent in your head, unaware of the body, so in trying to be present, alignment is important. Breathing helps you do that.

The other way to easily come into the present is by being in nature. Walking by a stream, watching clouds float in the sky, tuning in to the sounds of birds singing, seeing the sun set with changing colors. When you focus on nature and really tune in or feel the rhythm of what is around you, you naturally come into the present. For city dwellers, I always recommend connecting to the sky or finding a tree to sit against, actually feeling the energy that is present. If you can practice using nature to bring you into the present moment, then when you don't have access to the outdoors, you will still be able to re-create the sensation again using images. The goal here is to develop a strong sense of when you are present, nourished, and alive, and when you are not.

Remember, you are like an instrument through which information from your Soul can flow. Your ability to open up to receive guidance will be restricted if you aren't able to be present. Being cluttered with the past and future means you cannot hear guidance in the present.

Most of your suffering comes from being in the past or future, not the present. In sessions with clients, we always start by coming into the present, breathing deeply for a few moments and re-creating images of nature. If we don't do this, the session will not be as productive and creative possibilities will be limited. Creative work relies on you being fully present—releasing emotions, analysis, past memories, and future worries.

Again, remember the benefit of being present—you can hear your own inner guidance, you will feel energized and more alive, and you will, over time, feel more in tune with your own Soul, every day.

A long time ago, I had traveled out of town to conduct a workshop. My life partner had joined me, since part of the trip was for pleasure. The night before the workshop, he and I had a huge disagreement, one of the most distressing missteps that could end any relationship. The event was so significant that I actually ended the relationship, sending him on his way the very morning I was to handle a large group for a two-day event. Most people would have been very upset by this occurrence and that energy would have negatively influenced the event at hand. They would have had less energy or motivation to go on. Since I had been living this concept of the present moment, I was quite able to shift from the moment with him to the professional moment. Reliving that argument, the way it occurred, and the result—as well as all the moments of our relationship—would have taken me into the past. Thinking about the future, our upcoming plans, the fear of being alone again, and the sorrow of the loss would have taken me into the future. I consciously chose to stay in the present, focusing my attention on the "now." I needed all my energy for the workshop, and I knew how to stay out of the mind clutter, the monkey mind, of what I had just done. The net result was a terrific workshop where significant healing took place. I was as energized as those attending.

Once the event was over, I shifted my focus to him. While some may say I blocked out one event for another, that's not the case at all. There was no restricted sense of forcing one feeling or denying another. I was alive, excited, energized, and very much in the room with the attendees, just as jazzed by the work as I would have been if my personal life hadn't been disrupted. When you are in the present moment and not faking it, you feel strengthened, vital, and nourished. The sensation is very real, and the result is very positive. Creation occurs. There is no exhaustion.

Next time you wonder how to be present, remember the animals. If you're lucky enough to have one in your life, watch him or her. They are so alert, so vibrant, and so easy to be around because they are not weighed down by their minds. *They trust the life force within them. They flow with the energy around them. They are truly present for whatever is next, not anticipating, not judging, not analyzing.* All animals offer great lessons for being in the world. I am so grateful that each day, when they greet me with such joy, I'm reminded that they're seeing me for the first time. If we could all embody the present moment, what celebrations we would have!

CHECKPOINTS: *Where Are You Now?*

- Right now, try the fifteen-minute Present Moment Olympics. Well, what happened?
- On any given day, what percent of your time do you spend thinking about past events?
- What percent of your time do you spend on future occurrences?
- And, honestly, what percent do you spend on the present?
- To understand how your energy differs, remember a past moment when you were very, very fearful. Remember all the details. Notice how you feel.
- Now focus back in the moment of reading this. How has your energy been affected by going into the past?
- Who is in your life that focuses on the past? Or focuses on the future? What happens to you when you are around them?
- What are you willing to do to stay present?

Principles for Reflection

Work with these principles:

- *The present moment is the most fundamental key to unlocking your connection to your Soul. The energy you feel from living in the present is nourishing, healing, and regenerative.*

- *You are a life force of energy that you focus in various ways each moment. When you are focused on the past, that energy is not available in the current moment. You have engaged it elsewhere. And the same is true when you focus on the future.*

- *When you want to tune in and hear your Soul's guidance, it's very hard to do if you are everywhere but in the moment.*

- *Your past is not who you are today. Your past only matters if it's helping you become who you want to be today.*

- *The present moment is all about growth. If you show up, with all your energy for everything in life, then you will be nourished and satisfied.*

- *The present moment is a place of creation. Your energetic force is powerful when you are aligned. You can feel the difference. If you're feeling stressed, overwhelmed, disheartened, agitated, or worried, you are not in the present.*

- *Living a life of Everyday Soul means becoming aware of where your energy is going so that you can effectively tune in to present situations with your full life force.*

- *We are very unskilled at being in the present moment. This will require a new focus, one you will need to develop.*

- *Remember, you are like an instrument through which information from your Soul can flow. Your ability to open up to receive guidance will be restricted if you aren't able to be present. Being cluttered with the past and future means you cannot hear guidance in the present.*

- *Remember the benefit of being present—you can hear your own inner guidance, you will feel energized and more alive, and you will, over time, feel more in tune with your own Soul, every day.*

CHAPTER SEVEN

Fear

The Myth and the Trap

INSPIRATION

Our worst fear is not that we are inadequate. Our deepest fear is that we are powerful beyond measure. It is our light, not our darkness, that most frightens us. We ask ourselves, "Who am I to be brilliant, gorgeous, talented, and fabulous?" Actually, who are you not to be?
You are a child of God; your playing small doesn't serve the world.

NELSON MANDELA

Fear is not real.

It is the signal to go deeper and uncover what is trying to heal.

It is only a state of being, an energy, an actual, physical, tangible sensation in your body.

SO WHY DON'T YOU KNOW THAT?

I'm not saying you don't feel or experience fear, I'm just saying it's not the truth.

Before you say fear is a real emotion, I want you to think about a few things:

Ever had an overwhelming, debilitating fear of speaking in front of people? Then you spoke and it was gone?

Ever been gripped by the terror of thinking someone you love had been in an accident, then they came home and your fear was gone?

Ever have the fear that you were going to be fired for something you did? Amidst sleepless nights, you started rehearsing your defense and planning your résumé, but you weren't fired, and the fear went away?

You can make your own list. Even on the very day you're reading this book, nine times out of ten, you've experienced some fear, then *it was gone*. That's why fear is a lie. Once you're aware that fear occurs and yet disappears, then it's logical to be suspicious of what's real and what is not. Even if you were taught that fear is one of your emotions, that's fine, but with a little scrutiny, you could assume there's more going on than meets the eye. As yourself: What is this thing that comes and goes at will? Why don't I seem to have any control over it?

How does it occur with some people and not others? And why is it so unpredictable?

There is a spiritual part of all of us that is much grander than the human part. It knows when we are preventing spiritual growth, so fear occurs to open a new door. Fear is merely a way to uncover something in you that has been hidden. It is a door to healing your pain.

One of my clients is a six-figure earner, wears Chanel suits, drives a Saab, and fearlessly takes on any challenge. She's determined to go after life. But she feels less-than-successful in relationships. After a failed marriage, she's confused about trusting love and she's sworn she'll never get hurt again. Enter FEAR—a constant "red alert" underlying every encounter. "Don't hurt me, don't come close, I can't take the pain." Over and over, her heart stayed closed. She was literally trapping herself in the fear.

Thankfully, for her, her inner voice grew louder and she was listening. She was working to observe the fear, her behavior, and see why her life was "stuck" in this one area. She began uncovering clues to the origin of her fear. She acted on what she uncovered. Rather than reacting defensively to men, she consciously chose to be open, no matter how vulnerable this made her feel. She managed her fear. This was a brave decision.

She began trusting her heart. There was a true "knowing" that the fear was triggered from the past, not the present.

She experienced a new passion and sense of herself. She effectively reframed her fear. Her commitment to choose consciousness, manage her self-doubt of ever being loved, and choose to trust in herself and something greater created a completely new approach to living. She is now dating men who interest her and feeling she can show them both her femininity and her strengths, without automatically being hurt.

Investigating Your Fears

This woman's story captures the essence of how consciousness works. The rational mind will evaluate the risk, consider past history as evidence, and rationalize that the pain is intolerable. The fear is then trapped as the truth. While it may "feel" true, a conscious awareness allows you to dig deeper, uncover *where* the fear first originated, *how* often it repeats, *when* you actually create the expectation of pain, *whose* voice you are hearing, *why* you doubt yourself, and *what* you do automatically, negating any other result.

This is the process that shifts you out of fear and into the search for a new action.

Fear could be considered a natural part of being human. It seems to be an automatic reaction. When fear hits we respond—

fight or flight. This supposedly "natural" reaction has been described as an animal response, well documented by scientists.

But if we are to believe that an "animal" nature is who we are, then where is our higher intelligence, the higher mind? Isn't it possible that we have a different choice than animals? This is the point.

> *At the exact moment that you feel fearful, you can choose to consciously create that experience from a different perspective—a different vibration, a higher vibration. Not from the instantaneous level of animal reaction, but from your Soul.*

Using the higher intelligence you've been given is a new way to live in the world. This is not about traditional analysis. I'm referring to a greater conscious awareness through your mind, senses, heart, and Soul.

> *The main objective is to be responsible for healing fears that limit you.*

When you're afraid, there is panic in your reaction. You are literally gripped by fear—physically, emotionally, and mentally. It is a form of pain. The desire to remove the fear, deny the fear, or run from the fear occurs. We've been taught to avoid pain. So even the most intelligent person succumbs to fight or flight.

But you are *not* gripped spiritually. The Soul connection links you with *inner knowing, beyond fear.* Your conscious awareness accesses your "inner knowing" as you manage your reactions. You neutrally observe yourself, which allows you to stay conscious, evaluate everything honestly, and listen to your inner wisdom for true guidance.

The Miracle of Fear

The very moment when you feel fear is the moment to expect a miracle. Fear is a clue that you're on track. You are uncovering a part of yourself that is ready to heal. It is time for you to bring conscious understanding to deep, hidden pain, or it is time for you to uncover new talents and bring them into the world.

For a while, your inner voice and your fear are closely intertwined. As you "hear" your own guidance, you're less likely to believe in the fears automatically. As you trust more of what you "know," the fears become even less powerful. And once you use fear as a signal to go "inside yourself" to find the truth, then fear is just a state of being.

*Fear no longer limits you. You see fear as a sign for growth,
for learning, for change.*

Change is merely your soul talking to you. It is not something that happens *to* you, it is something *in* you that is happening. The external result is your signal to ask, "What do I
need to learn here? Why is this happening? What is the truth I
need to see?"

*Our ability to learn and grow becomes the focus of our
energy. We no longer want to be limited by fear.*

We face whatever we have to face, responsibly heal the
wounds, clean up the damage, and *fear-less-ly* follow our inner
voice, which knows what is best for our highest good.

Fear is not the boogeyman of our childhood, it is not the
tragedy that brings us to our knees. Fear is an energy that signals growth. That is all it is about. We define what fear means,
and we buy in to the idea that we must, at all costs, avoid feeling fear. We believe our fears are insurmountable and yet, time
after time, we can learn differently. But we don't readjust our
perspective on fear.

Accept that fear is natural to your nature and your conditioning. Everything around you reminds you to fear death, yet

in other cultures death is celebrated. Everything around you reminds you to fear loss, yet isn't loss the opportunity for a beginning, not an ending? Everything around you reminds you to fear crime, yet isn't crime just a loud signal asking us to focus on healing damaged people?

You are conditioned to experience fear in certain ways. Remember that the television you watch, the people you spend time with, and the thoughts you have all influence how you experience fear. Are you consciously choosing what's best for you?

And, most important, you choose your reaction to fear.

Denial, anger, paralysis, or acceptance, examination, and understanding—your conscious awareness influences how you understand fear.

Whether you choose to understand your own Soul and the inner wisdom you already have is your choice. Either way, you *will* experience fear. You can choose to manage fear consciously or not manage fear at all. If you choose not to, you'll feel "thrown around" by life, wondering why things are happening to you, and eventually you'll create a victim mentality— *Why me?* If this sounds familiar, you're already in the FEAR TRAP.

On the other hand, if you choose consciousness, you manage fears differently when they occur. You trust an inner Soul connection and you *know* exactly what to do that's best for you. You understand the fearful (animal) side of your nature will always react, but the higher intelligence you've been given can be aware of what's really true. Fear is just an energy moving through your body.

Here's a plan to help you tackle your fears and shed light on them so you can see the truth and release them:

1. **Get the facts about your fears.**

Be your own investigative reporter committed to the relentless pursuit of truth. When you find yourself fearful, check if you're remembering a past event, worrying about the future, or actually in the present moment. Most of the time, your fear has *nothing* to do with the present situation. Take a moment to question your feelings and try to break down into pieces what's causing your feelings. If you don't investigate the fears, you'll remain paralyzed and unable to act.

2. **Detach from your emotions.**

You're after the truth, not smoke and mirrors. This is your life. . . . Live in the dark or wake up and go after the truth.

Shine some light on what's been hidden and you'll see clearly. Your emotions are just an energy, not who you are.

I'm not saying deny your emotions, I'm saying detach. That means step aside, view what is happening, don't judge anything, make notes and learn why, when, how, what, who, where. You're looking for clues about your feelings. Why are you feeling this way? When did it start? How does this fear happen? What triggers it? Who is connected to the fear? Where do you feel fear? When does it recur?

3. Buy yourself a notebook and you're in business.

Keep notes on what you learn about yourself. You are re-creating who you are, so it's as if you'll need to learn about your fears for the first time. If you take time to jot down notes when you experience fear, you'll begin to see recurring patterns or themes, which then frees you to work on them more objectively. Taking notes brings greater awareness of your actions and reactions and, while it may seem tedious, it's actually worth the time to "go to school" on yourself. After all, it's your life you are trying to improve.

Here's a brief illustration of how awareness works to alleviate fear. Since my thirties, I'd always made good money and felt great pride in being free of money fears. Yet, when jobs ended, I found myself agitated, restless, and worried. This is probably a natural state when you're unemployed, but it was not a reaction founded on facts. Finding work had never been a problem, so what was really causing this fear to surface? First, I had to keep reminding myself to check on the feeling of fear. Was it from the past? Worries about the future, or what? Then I had to reread my notes on other times I'd felt this unsettling feeling of dread and hopelessness. It always recurred around money. And, last, I had to stay very calm as I viewed my life during a time when fear was keeping me awake at night, causing me to doubt myself, and creating a very disturbing level of anxiety. I had to detach from all that emotion to uncover the facts.

What I found was incredibly helpful. My fear—supposedly based on a fear of not having any money—had nothing to do with money at all. Makes sense, right? I'd always earned plenty of money (this was a fact). Instead, my fear was about control, specifically being out of control. I felt powerless. This sensation started in my childhood when my mother and father divorced. Without a stable source of income any longer, my mother panicked and created a sea of fear about what would happen to us (this was the past). I integrated all that fear about money into a promise to myself never to be in a position where anyone could control my life, as she had been (this was the future). As I realized that this promise actually triggered fear in me—being out of control—I began to learn to let go. The sense of "control" was artificially created from a childhood situation anyway.

I was now an adult, yet the panic from childhood affected my energy. Bringing this into my consciousness was the first step to releasing it. I could rationally understand that today (the present moment) was not the past. Sounds easy enough—but most of us get trapped by fears from the past.

> *Uncovering the root of your fear is the first step to releasing it.*

The Grip of Fear

Fear is like a spiral that you unwind. The most logical rationale for the fear will occur to you first. But as you dig deeper you will uncover very primitive feelings—of being unwanted or unloved, fear of dying, being hurt or abandoned—basic emotions that occur early in life when we cannot rationally explain why we feel what we feel. These sensations become trapped as reference points within us. Without consciousness, you utilize these same feelings as the "truth" of what you feel today. That's why fear feels so potent. It's never been evaluated in the light of a balanced perspective.

You may be surprised that such primal fear carries the energy it does. Some people experience the depth of pain that originally occurred when the fear happened. They may cry deeply, become furious, or withdraw numbly. Whatever you find that seems so "terrifying" won't stay that way once you bring it out into the open, in present time. Uncovering the original fear releases the energetic block, the "charge." Then you can begin clarifying why you had the reaction and how you want to adjust the way you carry it into your current life.

Trust that you have the ability to heal yourself, using your inner wisdom. If at any time you feel too overwhelmed physically, emotionally, or mentally, then consider resources and support that can help you. Reaching out to counselors, psychiatrists, twelve-step groups, past-life therapists, energy healers, friends, or family is part of exercising your conscious choice. We now have many, many options at our disposal for consciously managing the process of uncovering fear.

The main objective is to be responsible for healing fears that limit you.

Ever notice two people in a disagreement? They are a perfect example of being blocked. They are trapped in an emotional, energetic state where neither can be heard. Neither wants to change his or her point of view and neither realizes what's truly happening. Go beyond their words and no matter what they're saying, you will always uncover the main emotion—fear. They may be afraid of losing control or of being unloved or unwanted. Whatever they say, just know that their argument is about FEAR, not anything else.

If neither chooses to develop a conscious awareness of what is hidden in his or her fighting, the couple will never create the intimacy of trust needed in a loving relationship. The instantaneous reaction to make the other person "wrong" will distance them from each other and from themselves. They won't uncover their "need" to protect themselves, which means they'll be trapped, feeling misunderstood, isolated, angry, or hurt. Ultimately, they will reject the relationship.

When you realize how many times a day people are locked in situations like this, in homes and offices all over the world, it's amazing to think we ever use our higher intelligence. You have to wonder: *Who's in charge here—the adult or the child-like fears?* Without consciousness, the fear wins. We are energetic beings, with a mind–body–heart–spirit connection that impacts what we experience. If we don't investigate how fear locks us into limiting patterns, we are doomed to repeat them. Instead, we could learn whatever we need to learn to change the belief. Then challenge ourselves to stretch beyond what makes us uncomfortable.

So it's important to *tempt* your fears. This is the way you will grow as a human being. This is how you will understand who you are and who you want to become.

Always be gentle with yourself. There is no value in crashing through fear. It's not about being tough and "pushing through" everything. It is about learning more deeply about yourself, to release whatever is limiting you. Fear is a real sensation you experience physically, mentally, and emotionally. Be compassionate in understanding yourself. Accept the responsibility of improving yourself, bravely unearthing whatever lies exist.

A Signal to Grow

Start listening to your Soul's desire for you to grow. You will experience fear, but you will also feel the longing to keep growing, creating something new within yourself. The more you can identify how fear works, the clearer you will become about the decisions you make to stimulate that growing process.

Another client I coach had a few important relationships in her life, but in general nothing had been steady. She was in her early fifties. A real, loving relationship never seemed to stick. After significant work on her fears—intimacy, control, being unloved—she recognized one core fear that occurred every time a partner got involved with his work: She felt abandoned. This is how it showed up for her: She became edgy, agitated for no reason, unable to focus on her work, lost sleep, and had nausea and stomachaches. She began to worry (fear) about where he was, why he wasn't calling, and if he still liked her. This was a torturous cycle of fear that negatively impacted her life. She could get trapped if she was not conscious.

Before she unlocked her fear of abandonment, she usually instigated a fight, which caused them to split. She'd done this many times before. Her fear of what was going to happen would lead it to happen. That's how fear works.

You are energetically trapped in the emotional sensations that allow you to justify actions that prove your fears are right. Then you confirm that the fear is real. But it's not—if you unlock the mystery.

She had repeated this pattern so many times that she recognized what was coming—before it was too late. Now when she experiences that panic feeling, she meditates, breathes deeply, chuckles over this childlike fear, reads a spiritual book, and talks to her partner about the feelings she's having. She knows this helps her manage the fear and release the "charge" of the blocked energy. The fear never traps her.

The main understanding is this:

Fear is not the truth about who you are.

Fear exists all around us and will continue to exist, so you have to be prepared for how you want to survive in a fear-based world. You decide whether to focus your time and energy on personal growth work. You decide if your Soul is something you want to invest energy in discovering.

Spend some time looking at what's available today—books, tapes, seminars, people—"tune in" to what you're drawn to. Your inner wisdom will lead you to look in the place that's best for you. Whenever I work with someone who is just beginning spiritual growth work, I suggest he or she literally stand in front of the area in the bookstore dedicated to New Age, metaphysics, and self-help topics, scan what's there and listen. Your inner voice will speak to you. Trust that you know what's needed, beyond the rational mind. You do.

This same approach applies in every area of your life. Place yourself in situations—stores, social events, scenic settings, museums, dance classes, art galleries—see what you're led to explore. This is the conscious way to learn about your Soul. Let go of what you "should" or "shouldn't" do; try everything. Reignite the energy of discovery. If you tackle your own growth and learning with the same energy you use to avoid pain (fear), you will truly re-create your life.

Choosing growth over stagnation is the reason you are here.

Go to God and pray for the truth to shatter the lies. Ask sincerely to see and know the real fear. And you will.

Fear is merely a signal to uncover what has been hidden.

CHECKPOINTS: *Where Are You Now?*

- When you chose the work you did, what worried you?
- How often do you have restless nights of anxiety? When? Why?
- When do you trust your decisions, and when don't you?
- If you examine your life now, what do you fear will have to change?
- What person or situation stimulates your self-doubt?
- How often did your mother worry about money, your future, the family?
- How do you challenge yourself to learn something new?
- What fear did your parents pass on to you—success or failure?
- When you read the news on current events, what's your fear?
- When you were a child and felt fear, what did you pretend?
- How often and under what circumstances do you experience joy?

- What's your greatest fear for your children or your partner?
- Tap into the most critical part of yourself; what fear do you keep hearing?
- How often do you use your intuition, on a scale of 1 to 10?
- When have you been fearless in your life? Why? How did it occur?

Principles for Reflection

Work with these principles:

- *There is a spiritual part of all of us that is much grander than the human part. It knows when we are preventing spiritual growth, so fear occurs to open a new door. Fear is merely a way to uncover something in you that has been hidden. It is a door to healing your pain.*

- *At the exact moment you feel fearful, you can choose to consciously create that experience from a different perspective—a different vibration, a higher vibration. Not from the instantaneous level of animal reaction, but from your Soul.*

- *The very moment when you feel fear is the moment to expect a miracle. Fear is a clue that you're on track. You are uncovering a part of yourself that is ready to heal. It is time for you to bring conscious understanding to deep, hidden pain, or it is time for you to uncover new talents and bring them into the world.*

- *Fear no longer limits you. You see fear as a sign for growth, for learning, for change. Our ability to learn and grow becomes the focus of our energy. We no longer want to be limited by fear.*

- *The main objective is to be responsible for healing fears that limit you.*

CHAPTER EIGHT

*H*EALING

Let the Universe Support You

INSPIRATION
To live is the rarest thing in the world.
Most people exist, that is all.

OSCAR WILDE

The Little Book of Everyday Soul offers principles that help direct you to a more clear connection with your Soul. Each chapter provides a piece of the puzzle of a new orientation, that when put together, is like a mosaic, creating a new life. This chapter is important to restructuring your beliefs so that you can trust that the universe is supporting you. Developing this fundamental trust accelerates your experience of your own Soul and the guidance that is available to you.

The principle of healing is profound. Look around for clues and you'll see the truth loud and clear. Where there is a fire, there will eventually be green sprouts of grass; where there is a cut, the skin repairs itself.

The flow of healing happens when there is no resistance, when the natural order of events can occur easily. Because everything is always in a natural state of healing.

When you live your life connected to your Soul, you know this is as true for you personally as it is for the cut on your hand. You are healing, too. Whatever is in your past or in your current life has a chance to heal because that is the principle operating in all of life. Why would you be excluded?

There is always an opportunity for healing. We choose to accept this or not.

Our culture is only beginning to understand intuitive medicine, where healers can read or intuit illness in the body to help doctors better diagnose unsolved sickness. Now a more common practice, it was only recently that we even began to understand the relationship between our mental state and our physical state.

We are beginning to realize that we impact our health with our beliefs and approach to life. Most doctors will tell you that a patient diagnosed with a terminal illness will live longer if he or she wants to—and for no other factual reason. It is the patient's mental orientation that makes the difference. Medical conditions are only one piece of the puzzle of sickness. As spiritual beings, we are the other part. (For more information on this, read Caroline Myss, author of *Energy Anatomy* and *Anatomy of the Spirit*.)

But this chapter is not about physical illness. It is about your connection to your Soul, and accepting the grace of healing that is naturally available to you. Without any effort on your part, your body, your heart, and your mind want to heal and release suffering. It is not your Soul's intention for you to suffer. The objective is for you to heal.

Healing is the same as growing, moving beyond wounds and obstacles that restrict you so you can live fully to your potential with all of your gifts coming into the world.

The difficult part of healing comes from the fact that we do not take responsibility for it. We fail to realize the role we play in our own healing and that of others around us.

*Our thoughts, words, and actions carry energy that has
the potential to heal or harm. We choose what we send out.
When you understand the natural cycle of healing, you
begin to spot when you are resisting or blocking that
natural order of events.*

Ask yourself, Why do I choose sickness? Where is the healing in the sickness? Why do I choose anger or hatred? Where is the healing in those emotions? Why do I choose confusion, frustration, and complacency? Where is the healing in those?

Healing is possible, with or without our awareness. The difference is that we can assist the healing process by understanding what we need to do differently.

Healing creates an awareness of how we need to change.

A number of clients have come to me after experiencing difficult illnesses, situations that actually forced them to reexamine their lives and re-create a new plan. They wisely recognized that the illness was an indication that their lives were out of order, that something wasn't working right. Even when they'd "known it all along," it was the illness that catalyzed them to make changes.

The question for each of us who are not experiencing serious illness is whether we, too, need to make changes and are resisting doing so. Does it take a major health challenge for the healing to really begin? In other words, the outer body illness is merely reflecting some other dysfunction in life that wants to heal. Why do we have to wait for that to happen?

If the natural order of life is for healing to occur, then whenever you are out of alignment, something will "break down" in order for you to take steps to adjust what's awry. Sickness is not the only indicator of the need for healing. Very often, clients experience a trauma in their professional lives. They are fired or let go.

When this happens, they typically feel embarrassed, labeling themselves failures on some level. Yet the truth is, more often than not, if you check back with these people years later, they will always tell you that the incident was the best thing that could have happened to them. Thanks to the firing, they went on to do the very thing they'd always wanted to do but didn't have the courage to act on. I hear this all the time.

So why do we misunderstand the "bad" things that happen to us and take them for face value, as if something has gone wrong, when in fact it's the natural order of healing? Mainly, it's because we've never been taught the concept of healing, as it relates to alignment of mind, body, and soul.

If you've lived a life out of alignment, unconnected to your Soul, a breakdown somewhere in your life is usually a chance to reconnect differently. It's your opportunity to find your Soul and re-create a life from a deeper level of being. Some may call it a "wake-up call." Whatever you call it, it's your chance to check what you've been doing to see if changes are in order.

Healing Is Natural

As you consider the principle of healing, keep asking yourself, *What do I need to heal to be free of suffering?* If you ask this question, an answer will come. In the chapter on Love, I mentioned that I knew I needed to heal my heart, so rather than wait for a heart attack at an older age, I began facing my fears and issues to release the pain and suffering. Ask yourself this question and see what answer comes. What am I carrying as painful memories? Or fears? Or issues preventing me from fully living a joyful life?

Begin the questioning now to open the door for your own healing.

Another way to understand the premise of healing is to remember that your Soul knows what you want to accomplish. Your Soul knows your greatest heartfelt desire. Your Soul wants to help you. Yet often you create situations that prevent what you want from coming to you because of your fears. (Imagine if everything you really wanted happened right now. You'd probably become panic-stricken with all the change.)

Your Soul knows how to help you move closer to your heart's desire by assisting you during your "breakdowns." The assistance comes in the form of healing.

I find fascinating the difference between people and dogs when it comes to healing. As an intuitive coach and healer, I work with countless rescue dogs that have been physically and emotionally abused. They cower, submissively urinate, growl, or hide—yet somewhere in their eyes or behavior, you see the desire to trust a human again. They rarely give up on the remote possibility that we will care for them and that they can give their love to another human. Over time, working with dogs that have "issues," I know they will eventually make a choice to release that piece of history in favor of the present moment. It's my job to wait for that transition to happen and hold the possibility for them.

This is how it works with humans, too. Pain and suffering push you toward change and rebuilding trust and, like the dogs, you must choose at some point to commit to fully trusting again. Here's the big difference, though, one that is profound in the lessons it offers to those of us interested in personal growth: Dogs live in the present moment, so while they may remember something bad, once they realize the present is different, they allow themselves to heal. They do not hang on to their history. They accept the new gift of healing and release the pain.

People, on the other hand—and that includes most clients I've dealt with—stay focused on the suffering and resist healing. They get caught in their past history and their future doubts and worries, so they miss the natural flow of healing energy. They hold on to their baggage. Just picture yourself heading to the airport with a bag for every issue you have . . . maybe you'd be lugging a twenty-three-piece set on your trip?

So how do you travel light? How do you release pain and suffering and really accept the natural order of healing that is available all the time on this planet? The answer is what this book is all about. First, acknowledge and develop an awareness of your Soul, and then learn to uncover whatever is in the way of growing that Soul connection.

Generally, it's your fears and beliefs that block the clear link to your Soul.

The dogs I work with don't carry the history of beliefs and fears in the same way, so they are more free to shift and transition to a new life. We are always amazed by dogs that have been truly traumatized by humans, arriving at the farm and within days, are racing around, barking, playing, and loving us, as if nothing had ever happened to them.

Dogs shift quickly because they do not resist healing. You can do the same.

So what about you? Will you allow yourself to shift quickly and let go of your pain? Remember, your finger heals when it is cut. You may apply antiseptic ointment and a bandage, or even visit the emergency room if the cut is bad, but basically you do very little for the actual healing and regeneration of skin to occur. There is a natural flow of healing energy available to your body.

If you trust this is so and have seen examples yourself, then it's logical to ask what you can do to promote healing where you know there are other wounds. Why wouldn't you be proactive in treating wounds from the past that haunt you and prevent you from living a more fulfilling life? Whether your wounds are physical or emotional, healing is possible. What's required is that you choose to allow it.

Healing Can Be Simple

If you're wondering what to do to promote healing, that's good, because when you focus in this direction, the universe can then support you with experiences and people. You naturally attract what you need to heal. Out of the blue, someone will enter your life offering exactly what you need. In fact, if you're reading this book, you probably have people and experiences in your life already that are doing this right now.

On the other hand, if you block this concept and resist, suffering continues and very little that is helpful can find its way to you. Instead, you actually create more pain for yourself. Eventually, the pain becomes unbearable, which leads you to reach out and admit the need for healing. For some people, it is only then that they allow healing to occur.

Rather than endure that level of trauma, why not embrace the principles of growth and healing? Like the rescue dogs, just move on with your life, shifting into a new awareness of what is possible. They have no resistance to healing, why would you?

One of the easiest ways to foster your own healing is by being in nature. I mean, literally, *being* in nature. Find a tree, a meadow, a lake, a sunset—whatever speaks to you and *be there*. Learn to quiet the mind with breathing and digest the rhythm of nature as it unfolds with you as part of it. If you're used to chaos and city energy, this may take some time to experience. Remember that you have all the time in the world to grow, once you've committed to healing. Plus, everything will accelerate the more you believe this is the point of why you are here.

> *You are here to heal the wounds and grow to your fullest potential.*

Whenever clients come to me asking for clarity or new direction, I always advise that they spend more time *in* nature. Really in nature. Walk with the intent of just walking, not thinking about your day or your problems. Instead, really walk on the earth, feeling the sun, the wind, and the chattering of little creatures that you normally overlook.

I also always recommend serious practice with breathing. Deep breathing, where you allow the oxygen to nourish you, actually focusing on each breath as the "breath of life." You have the power to give this to yourself when you focus on the magnificence of this involuntary miracle—breathing. So find a spot to sit or walk and just breathe with the intent of giving yourself life. The more you focus on breathing, the easier it is to let go of the mind noise.

The breath is a miracle tool for healing. It is your job to focus on using it to its fullest rather than ignoring what occurs so naturally. Remember, the breath is a sign of support from the universe.

Did you have to do anything to deserve that vote of confidence? No, you have been given this grace because you are here, alive at this moment, in a body.

One client developed a practice of breathing deeply before every meeting and before he heads home so that when he's home with his family, he's truly in the present moment with them and not in his head and the day's events. He began to see more clearly the power of the breath in healing all aspects of his own pain, as well as the turmoil in his interactions with people. He was more often present, rather than focused on the past or future, which meant that he experienced people in a profoundly different way. As I said to him, if you want to heal your life (which makes sense), then utilize the tools you have been given.

The combination of being in nature and concentrating on your breath is powerful. If you really commit to a program of outdoor time with trees, birds, wind, and sun, just breathing, you will see your life shift in a new direction that is more nourishing for you.

What happens is that you change your inner rhythm; it becomes more natural. You start to breathe *with* the earth. Rather than breathing at the pace of an intense, crowded, rushed city life, you begin resonating with all that is *alive*. Your vibration begins to match the larger energy of the universe, which is always about *growth*. Even in decaying trees, there is growth for the evolution of the tree to the next season. The same is true for you.

> *And when your rhythm is more natural, you begin to resonate with everything around you and especially with what's inside of you, which is your Soul.*

In searching for a connection to my own Soul and a more meaningful life, I had to make transitions time after time: from city life in New York and Los Angeles to a more suburban country life in Connecticut. As I look back, I can see that each change was a step toward today, where all I experience is the unbridled power of nature. Living on 183 acres is a far cry from a townhouse in crowded Marina del Rey or the eleventh floor of a doorman-staffed building in New York. Even my little cottage in Cos Cob, Connecticut, was jammed between other houses, neighbors, cars, and noise that often overshadowed whatever nature was nearby.

Yet I know that I could never have jumped from city life to living in rural America without transitions. My belief structure had to change—which is what I'm sharing in this book. My experiences of connecting to my Soul had to grow so I could jump courageously even further from what seemed normal. And I had to clearly and loudly feel and hear my own inner guidance. That meant I had to quiet the noise and clutter around me so that inner and outer were one in harmony. My own inner rhythm matched the outer rhythm. I needed a great deal of healing to grow into this moment in time.

For most of us, this is a lifetime's work. It is an "unfolding" of who you really are, from the inside out. Eventually, the outer world will accurately reflect who you are—you will live a life that is satisfying and rich with wonder.

But it's important to remember that this is a process. Even your injured finger doesn't heal overnight. Time is part of what is needed for healing and growth. Take some clues from nature. The seasons change. There is a flow to what occurs, with energy moving naturally to create the changes we see. All that growth is continual and natural. You, too, have the opportunity to move with that type of flowing energy. The big difference between you and the trees that change from winter to spring to summer to fall is that they do not resist—they allow the growth and healing energy to move through them. You can do the same.

Your Belief Matters

Healing is far greater than the limited definition we're given most of our lives, that of getting well. What is "well" only stems from our perspective of good and bad. There is no good or bad, no right or wrong in growth, only healing so more growth may happen.

Let go of the results. Trust that the perfect healing is taking place right now. It may even be death. There is no good or bad when you can see the tremendous potential for healing. Death may be the most positive end result of healing.

Illness or ill will suggests a readiness for healing, a healing opening. We choose to create a crisis or simply uncover what needs to be healed. Reach out for ways to help yourself heal. Never accept that healing is not possible.

Look for what is being healed at all times, despite the outcome. Always check to see if you are interfering with the natural healing process. If so, change whatever you are doing.

Hold the belief that healing is natural.

CHECKPOINTS: *Where Are You Now?*

- What needs to be healed? Where is your pain blocked?
- How afraid are you of letting go of that pain? Have you become so comfortable with this situation that suffering is what feels right?
- How do you allow yourself to grow now—with anger and pain? Or with easy changes?
- Can you remember an example or situation where healing simply happened?

Principles for Reflection

Work with these principles:

- *The flow of healing happens when there is no resistance, when the natural order of events can easily occur. Because everything is always in a natural state of healing.*

- *There is always an opportunity for healing. We choose to accept this or not.*

- *Healing is the same as growing, moving beyond wounds and obstacles that restrict you so you can live fully to your potential with all of your gifts coming into the world.*

- *Our thoughts, words, and actions carry energy that has the potential to heal or harm. We choose what we send out. When you understand the natural cycle of healing, you begin to spot when you are resisting or blocking that natural order of events.*

- *Healing creates an awareness of how we need to change.*

- *Your Soul knows how to help you move closer to your heart's desire by assisting you during your "break-downs." The assistance comes in the form of healing.*

- *Generally, it's your fears and beliefs that block the clear link to your Soul.*

- *Dogs shift quickly because they do not resist healing. You can do the same.*

- *You are here to heal the wounds and grow to your fullest potential.*

- *The breath is a miracle tool for healing. It is your job to focus on using it to its fullest rather than ignoring what occurs so naturally. Remember, the breath is a sign of support from the universe.*

- *When your rhythm is more natural, you begin to resonate with everything around you and especially with what's inside of you, which is your Soul.*

CHAPTER NINE

Divine Order
Redefining How You Trust

INSPIRATION
I want to know God's thoughts. The rest are details.

ALBERT EINSTEIN

Connecting with your Soul requires a new orientation toward trust. For most people, this is a dramatically different level of trust, what you might actually consider "a leap of faith" because what you're asking yourself to do is trust something you cannot see, something you have not previously relied on, and something you have no proof is real. You are trusting whatever *resonates within you*, rather than what you have been taught or learned to be true. This is a realignment of mind, body, *and* Soul.

When you receive guidance from within, that inner knowing requires you to trust yourself. When you open your heart fully to the energy of love, that requires you to trust yourself and others. When you accept the possibility of greater abundance in your life, that requires you to trust that your reality can change. When you trust that your own natural excellence will be rewarded, you must then act on your talents. When you trust the present moment, that means you must let go of worries and move ahead, without being able to see what's next.

> *Your ability to trust something greater than yourself is key. You begin trusting something beyond the obvious reality of day-to-day life. This greater intelligence and energy become available to you in what I call "Divine Order."*
>
> *There is a greater hand at work, with which you can* **CO-CREATE, IF YOU TRUST.**

To connect to your Soul fully, you must let go of all the learning that restricts you.

> *If you can embrace that there is a Divine Order to all that occurs, you will be able to let go more easily.*

So exactly what is Divine Order? First, ask yourself how things occur in life. What do you believe? Do you believe you make everything happen? Do you believe that what happens is fate? Do you believe it's a chaotic series of unrelated events?

What created the result called your life? Now, before you continue reading, take a moment to reflect on the twist of events that led to your various jobs, your marriage, where you live, the close friends you connect with, the hobbies you have. What made these things occur?

When I ask clients to reflect on the various turns in their life that led from one thing to another, usually they will notice a flow. It's as if things worked out for the best, even if at the time it didn't appear that would happen. Clients often mention a series of coincidences or connections that linked events together to create the end result. It's as if some assistance or guidance was involved that led them to do whatever they did. Have you felt this way, too?

When you seriously reflect on the chronology of events in your life, you'll see that your life is a bit like a series of building blocks, each moment connected to the next. Usually it all makes more sense in retrospect.

This order of events is Divine Order. There is a greater force at work for your own good, connecting what seem to you to be unrelated events. Yet, looking back, you can see the benefits in the way things flowed. Trusting that Divine Order is at work in your life requires a certain orientation in your beliefs.

No matter what is happening, your belief structure must carry this approach:

Everything is working perfectly.
I am in exactly the right spot at the right moment.
Everything works easily.
I am supported by something far greater than myself.

Imagine if your beliefs matched these words. Life would look quite different to you. There would be no sense of missed opportunities, no sense of mistakes, no sense that pain is an inevitable part of life, and no sense of being alone to figure it all out.

The way you now exist would substantially change.

Are you brave enough to consider that the way you think life works is not necessarily the truth of how life really works?

You are a co-creator with your Soul.

There is a way of being in life that welcomes the Divine Order of events. You actually flow with the events, rather than resist them. You know that what is occurring is blessed by something far greater than humans can imagine. This is not fate.

This is a divinity that has an overriding purpose—to help you move closer and closer to your Soul, to rediscover who you really are.

The options you choose to uncover are always up to you. That is the nature of "free will." But Divine Order is always at play.

Divine Order is how your Soul works with you to help you create your life.

How could you assume that you were *not* part of an ordered universe with a natural recurring rhythm of events? Just witness the cycle of the seasons, the amazing birthing patterns of whales year after year, the involuntary motions of breathing, the ebb and flow of the tides. Doesn't it feel natural that we, too, would have a pattern to living, a place in the universe with a certain synchronicity? This is Divine Order. It is the spirit part of us in action.

A client I've been coaching for more than two years had been working hard to balance her professional and personal lives. She longed for a child and a family, yet her work was so consuming that she found little time for a personal life, let alone time to meet anyone to date. While she had made great progress realigning her energy to a calmer approach, she knew she still had to let go of the frenetic work orientation to allow a man to enter her life. Her strong desire for a child was driving the desire to make more concerted adjustments in her life.

We focused on trust and her ability to understand Divine Order. We looked carefully at every milestone in her life to see how each event led to greater growth. She began to see how everything was building, moment by moment, year after year, to shape her life. Each relationship led to greater understanding about herself and what she truly wanted in her life. I asked her to let go of her expectations of each man she met, let go of the questioning about whether he was "the right one," and stop forcing a conclusion. Instead, I asked her to begin trusting that her Soul was directing who was sent to her. Honor the order of events as a way to help her grow, regardless whether the result was marriage. The outcome was not hers to control.

Like many people, she had never recognized the spiritual side of herself, her Soul, as being a co-creator of her life. She, in fact, had spent very little time learning about this inner part of herself, so she thought that she alone was "making everything happen." Her orientation was that if she didn't do it, it wouldn't get done. Yet, as she embraced the idea that her Soul could guide her to an appropriate partner, and through that "wiser" force or energy the events could unfold, she began to relax. She started changing her belief system to include the ideas that "everything was working perfectly" and "that she was in the right spot at the right time." This realignment in her trust of something greater than herself took time, but brought such a deep contentment that she knew she was on the right track.

We are all spiritual beings, and also physical, mental, and emotional humans. The breath of life still leaves us mystified. We are humbled by what we see on the planet that we cannot explain. The very nature of who we are is left unanswered after centuries of probing. The part of us we cannot explain or see or completely understand is the intangible spirit.

Understanding spirit requires us to relinquish our form of "knowing" for "not knowing." In the experience of not knowing, we understand creation, we hear our Souls, we welcome Divine Order.

If everything is working perfectly and you are in exactly the right place at the right time, then all you have to do is become aware of what's really happening—the "why" of what is happening. The more conscious you become of the order of events divinely created for you, the more able you are to heal, learn, and grow to another level of living. You trust Divine Order. You truly believe everything is working for your highest good, in your best interest.

If you can learn to trust that everything works for your highest good, your greatest growth, and your ultimate healing and understanding, then you will see the divinity in everything, no matter how it looks on the outside.

The female client who wanted a partner and a baby found herself sitting on an airplane two years ago. Her normal approach would have been to ignore the man next to her, pull out her laptop, and bury herself in work, assuming the person next to her was a nuisance not worthy of her time. But since we'd been working together and she'd agreed to stay open to the Divine Order of events, she responded to his interest in having a conversation. She kept her laptop closed and talked to him instead. Rolling forward, this single man became a serious relationship that led to the birth of her daughter, now two years old. She did not marry the man, but through her trust and openness and understanding, she now enjoys the child she had longed to have. And she knows that, in time, the appropriate man will follow.

For her, the order of events did not follow the structure of the typical family unit. Some people might have reacted with a sense of dismay and worry, facing the prospect of being a single mother. But it was her connection to her Soul that led her to know deep inside that this path was right for her. The child, not the man, was her deepest heart's desire, so she accepted what occurred with grace, blessed by the larger hand at work.

Here's another example of how Divine Order works and why trust is important to truly understand. About three years ago, I felt called to help rescue dogs. At first we did this in our home in urban Connecticut, placing sixty-five dogs into homes in a year and a half. While that was incredibly satisfying, I wanted to do more and longed to increase our efforts. I had prayed for many, many years to God—or what I consider the infinitely wise source of energy available to us—to put me on my purpose. I had longed for a purposeful life where I could be utilized in service to others. So when the idea of rescuing dogs came to fruition, it resonated within me so loudly, I knew I had to follow this path to its fullest.

Watching the various order of events in my life, inspired by the divine intervention present in each and every turn, I trusted more was to come, and that the dogs were part of the next step. My partner and I began looking for property that would allow at least twenty dogs on-site, as well as people visiting, a vacation camp for dog lovers, and room for inner-city kids to heal and grow, working with the rescued dogs. The vision was enormous, much larger than the four dogs we fostered each month out of our home. As we visited various properties, we finally found the "perfect" one in Massachusetts. We put money down, committed to a purchase, and were set to move in. Shortly thereafter, neighbors heard about our plans and began complaining, though we'd not yet moved in. After much chaos and confusion, it was clear we were not wanted there.

Crushed and sure the dream was gone, I kept looking for more properties, but felt uncertain of the outcome. It was at this moment I had to dig deep inside myself to remember example after example of how events work for my best good. All I really had to do was trust that our vision would allow a better property to reveal itself. In other words, I had to jump off the cliff, without seeing where I'd land, just trusting everything was working perfectly.

And, of course, that's exactly what happened. We now live in a very rural area where neighbors have no issues with barking dogs or a parade of cars. We have 183 acres that accommodate every aspect of our dream. We operate a doggie vacation camp every summer, an inner-city kids' program, and the rescue effort. By truly, sincerely trusting a Divine Order, I was able to let go of disappointment in losing the "perfect" property and receive what was actually more perfect than I could imagine.

Your Soul has a view of you that is vastly different from what you see from your own history.

Trusting Divine Order is about trusting events as they unfold, outside of your control. You actually release control and expect assistance. It's not about miracles; it's about options that you cannot imagine in your own mind, but that your Soul knows will work best for YOU. Your Soul has a far greater perspective on your life and the purpose of why you are here.

There is a gentleness in living with Divine Order as a principle of understanding what happens. There is less judgment, less self-criticism, and less criticism of others. Meanwhile, there is more flexibility, optimism, and appreciation for how the unexpected becomes reality. You begin to see the miracle of your individuality as a part of a far larger universe.

What is required is that you pay close attention to the world around you, assuming it has been completely customized for your greatest growth and clearest connection to your Soul. Through this understanding, you can more clearly see the meaning of your life.

Realign Your Beliefs

Getting started adjusting your beliefs requires that you focus in a new way. The following points will help you embrace new understanding in an orderly fashion so you can begin to shift your awareness.

EVERYTHING IS WORKING PERFECTLY.

Think about your reaction when things go wrong. How do you automatically view what's wrong? Do you have a feeling of dread? Does it seem destined to "not work out"? Do you feel unlucky? Or do you dismiss the negative event? Do you block the disappointment and assume an attitude of "better luck next time" and plow ahead?

If you look at your reaction at the moment things go wrong, you'll see the true beliefs that underlie how you create your life. If you embrace a Divine Order at work, your reactions are quite different. Nothing is ever wrong. *Nothing.* It may not match what you have in your head, but it's not wrong. You just trust that there is a realignment occurring on your behalf that will, in the end, be far better than you anticipated.

When something doesn't work the way you want it to work, you look for the grace within the change. You look for the blessing. Many times what comes to you is far better than you expect. Whatever challenges or surprises occur actually move you into a place of greater growth and understanding, and reshape who you are and what you want. Isn't your growth the most important thing?

Imagine if you knew everything that was going to happen to you in your life. Every event, every moment, every person you'd meet—everything. Wouldn't you feel stagnant and uninspired? In fact, bored? Instead, if you embrace the idea that you are co-creating with a higher wisdom and intelligence—God if you like—then it's obvious that growing is the main objective. You are stretched, stimulated, and inspired in new ways.

After sixteen years of producing television programs, I can tell you that I could predict the words, the shots, the music, and the people's reactions, which left me completely uninspired. Growing creatively had ended. I welcomed a greater force moving me to something new. Little did I know how dramatically different life would be. Or how much better. Thankfully, I trusted the turns and twists.

I AM IN EXACTLY THE RIGHT SPOT AT THE RIGHT MOMENT.

Have you ever longed for something, or felt there must be something else or somewhere else you should be? Have you ever looked at others and felt they were lucky when something good came their way—luckier than you? Does it seem like you are always just missing the chance at something good and someone else gets it? Or have you ever felt that sooner or later your luck would run out and things would come crashing down?

Again, look at your reactions to events to uncover the beliefs. It's these beliefs that prevent you from *flowing* with Divine Order. Instead, you resist what comes your way, creating pain and suffering.

If you'd been told that no matter where you are and what you're doing, you're exactly where you need to be, how much pressure would be lifted from you? Really imagine a day sensing that you are not doing anything wrong. There isn't something else you need to be doing. You don't need to change anything at all. This is very foreign to most of us, who have been raised to examine ourselves with scrutiny and are unforgiving of any imperfections. We endlessly compare ourselves to others, see flaws and faults, and feel less than adequate in our lives. There's always a nagging doubt that something better could be for us.

When you trust and live with Divine Order in your consciousness, you know that your Soul is guiding you. You are always guided. So rather than analyze, you just need to develop the ability to "tune" inside to hear that guidance. Once you do that, then you know you're exactly where you need to be at every moment. You can actually feel the co-creative process linked to your Soul. You feel more solid and trust that each moment is designed just for you. Each person you "coincidentally" meet, each experience you have, all tie together for your greater good and growth. A contentment comes with living this way—a deep satisfaction knowing there is no other place to be other than where you are each moment of your life.

EVERYTHING WORKS EASILY.

How often do you catch yourself thinking or saying, "This is going to be tough"? When something new is presented, do you first think of how hard it will be to accomplish? Do you sometimes feel everything is overwhelming and just too much to handle? Do you believe that without hard work nothing will happen? Do things seem difficult and take a long time to complete, drawn out with problems and obstacles? Do you ever feel like nothing good is ever easy?

Most of us would answer yes to these questions because we live in a culture that tells us that hard work is the way to succeed. The Protestant work ethic is based on the premise that good people work hard and are then rewarded. Plus, we live in a society that reveres people who overcome challenges and problems and still succeed. In other words, if you aren't making sacrifices and experiencing difficulties, then it's not worth doing. Success and victory come with a price. Or so we're taught. Again, this is just a belief, a group belief that we are taught is the truth.

Now challenge your belief with another way of being, trusting that a divine spiritual hand is at work. Wouldn't there be other options available? Why would difficulty be the only way to approach everything? Of course, there are other options with which to approach the order of events called your life. The most important is a belief that everything is easy. Try that on for a day and notice how often you fight it when things are easy. You are addicted to the struggle because it feels normal. So in order to really embrace the ease with which things happen in the spirit world, you'll have to *trust* that this is really possible. And then practice each day with the belief that easy is okay. Remember, your conditioning is to believe that difficulty is rewarded, that there must be something wrong if it's easy.

The truth is that nothing is hard for your Soul because there is no "hard." Only humans define things as easy or difficult. Your Soul sees your life as a platform for growing opportunities. If you embrace that concept, too, and accept that it's possible for growth to be easy, then there is a flow to life rather than resistance.

I AM SUPPORTED BY SOMETHING FAR GREATER THAN MYSELF.

Most of us assume that we have our families, friends, and ourselves and that's it.

We tend to forget that a stronger spiritual force is available to us. We may believe in religion and a God that is all empowered, but we have little relationship on a day-to-day basis with God in the details of our life. We sense that God is about creation on a big level, and not applicable to our mundane lives. Yet this is far from the truth. Once you resonate with your Soul and know that your spiritual energy is a part of everything you do, you no longer feel that sense of aloneness. You feel supported and guided.

Now, rather than disbelieve that this is possible, just practice acting as if it is. Give yourself the benefit of the doubt that possibly, just possibly, you are being held within a greater guidance system, for lack of a better word, that you can access whenever needed. Just like the trees and flowers and stars, you naturally have a powerful energy available to assist you in being.

All that is required to live this belief is to begin believing it's possible. Start looking for examples of when this happens. Notice how unexpected surprises occur.

If you can understand that you are not alone creating your life, then you will enjoy the treasure of gifts that come your way.

Divine Order is an unfamiliar concept that will take some practice to put into your life every day. But I challenge you to think about what belief is now guiding your orientation to life. If you aren't experiencing a Soulful connection to how you create your life, then how are you doing it? What is shaping the way you create your life? Divine Order is akin to grace. Something far greater than you is available to assist you. Why would you believe otherwise?

CHECKPOINTS: *Where Are You Now?*

- How hard is it to accept that you're not totally in charge of your life?
- What scares you about honoring a greater energy or intelligence?
- Is it possible just to try this belief system?
- What are you trusting now that shapes your life?

Principles for Reflection

Work with these principles:

- *Your ability to trust something greater than yourself is key. You begin trusting something beyond the obvious reality of day-to-day life. This greater intelligence and energy become available to you in what I call "Divine Order."*

- *There is a greater hand at work, with which you can CO-CREATE, IF YOU TRUST.*

- *If you can embrace that there is a Divine Order to all that occurs, you will be able to let go more easily.*

- *This is a divinity that has an overriding purpose—to help you move closer and closer to your Soul, to rediscover who you really are. Divine Order is how your Soul works with you to help you create your life.*

- *Trusting Divine Order is about trusting events as they unfold, outside of your control. You actually release control and expect assistance. It's not about miracles; it's about options that you cannot imagine in your own mind, but that your Soul knows will work best for YOU. Your Soul has a far greater perspective on your life and the purpose of why you are here.*

- *What is required is that you pay close attention to the world around you, assuming it has been completely customized for your greatest growth and clearest connection to your Soul. Through this understanding, you can more clearly see the meaning of your life.*

CHAPTER TEN

RESPONSIBILITY
Embrace the Grace

INSPIRATION
Live by Intuition and Inspiration
and let your whole life be a revelation.

EILEEN CADDY

Each of us has been given a lifetime that is ours and it is our individual birthright to bring our Soulfulness into being. The irony is that most of us have no clue that this deep, meaningful part of ourselves exists, and in fact many never fully engage in the search for the Soul within. If you choose to embrace the concepts of *The Little Book of Everyday Soul*, then it is your responsibility to yourself to search.

Your Soul is ever present, awaiting your acceptance of the wisdom and guidance available as your birthright. All you have to do is decide that this pursuit matters. But bear in mind that you and only you can make this decision. And only you can carry this desire to its most fruitful conclusion. There is no parent, no teacher, no cultural structure forcing you to walk this path toward a union with your Soul. In fact, there isn't much external support at all. But what awaits you is bountiful once you start and once you commit.

Many clients come to me wanting to develop themselves and experience more fulfillment in their lives, whether it be personal or professional, yet they often want it all to happen within the safety of what they know. That is actually not possible—and it's not the point. A deeper relationship with yourself requires that you let go enough to allow something new to develop. A true journey in which you are living this Everyday Soul experience is like surfing a great wave: There are exhilarating moments and those where you're truly under water, wondering where "up" is. Yet, for those who persist, commit, and take on the responsibility of this path, the rewards are immeasurable.

At forty-six, I sit in contentment and peace I had no idea I'd achieve. There were no guarantees, but I can assure you that what I've found anyone can find, and that the trip is worth every moment of anxiety and confusion and fear. In fact, these emotional reactions ensure that you are on the right track, that you're pushing beyond what is comfortable into areas of great growth. I made a decision at age thirty to "embrace the grace" of my Soul and move toward this union fully without being deterred. For whatever reason, I was clear that *this* pursuit was the most important focus for my life. I made my Soul my own responsibility to find and know.

In understanding responsibility, most of us are conditioned to think of it as a way of being a solid, good citizen: honest, trustworthy, and dependable. These descriptive terms are accurate, but they have nothing to do with the responsibility I am speaking of, specifically with respect to your Soul. What I am pointing to is the deep inner guidance of fulfilling your purpose here on Earth, being who you came to be. For some, that may be a mission of obvious service, for others it's flipping burgers at the local diner. Neither is better than the other if done with deep Soulfulness every day. Some of the most centered, heart-felt humans cross our paths in the most unlikely places, and we remember them as unique. Why do they stand out in your mind? What did you feel from them? What stirred inside of you that felt different? It was your Soul linking you to another's Soul. That's what we're here to do: express the way of the Soul with others.

Please remember that the union of Souls is not only about people, it's about animals and nature and all that is universally given to us as we breathe this air and walk this earth. We are uniting with the earth as we step on the soil and inhale the breath of life. Your opportunity to connect is endless and so exciting. To miss these moments of grace is a pity.

Yet most people living today miss most of what they are being given each day. What about you? What have you taken to heart in reading the *Little Book*? What will you put into practice? Is there something that you can hold on to in order to start this journey? Is there something you are eager to deepen even more?

Are you willing to be responsible for finding these answers? Will you be courageous with your life? Will you entrust your life to yourself, letting go of all the outer influences and "shoulds" that shape your decisions?

You Create Your Life

Very often, clients share with me situations that trouble them, usually someone or some occurrence where they feel they've been "wronged." Supposedly without reason, they feel slighted, cheated, or endangered, whether it's financially, professionally, or personally. Yet once you begin to relate to your life from the perspective of your Soul, you quickly take responsibility for all that exists.

What you have in your life you create.

This is an important belief to understand.

Nothing happens to you. You are not a victim. Instead, you are given opportunities to grow and wake up to a greater consciousness of what your life means.

The tests and difficulties are signals for you to wake up, to truly become aware of how you are creating whatever circumstances occur. What has been your role? What is the benefit of what is occurring? (Yes, negative situations have a benefit for you.) Where is the opportunity for growth?

A perfect example of this concept of responsibility comes through a few of my female clients. All single, all disappointed by the lack of love in their lives, all disheartened that something is wrong—with the men. Relationship after relationship, they experience the same result. Yet they spend time pointing fingers at the men, rarely recognizing the recurring themes as a signal to work on themselves. They miss the chance for healing because they are not taking responsibility for their own role in their lives. They look outside themselves rather than inside.

Once you entrust your life to a greater force of wisdom— your Soul—disappointments become clear indicators of areas for growth. Growth as in work on yourself.

It's time to ask, Where is healing needed? What beliefs are holding me back? Why is fear blocking this for me? What changes are needed within me?

> *This orientation of looking in the mirror is a responsible one, where you understand the dynamic principle——you create your life. Your life does not just happen to you. Your orientation creates what you experience.*
>
> *When you are connected to your Soul, you minimize a great deal of suffering because you are finally on course. Your life is aligned with the deepest part of you and what you came to do. The inside and the outside are in sync.*

Rather than a life focused on ego, personality, and dysfunction, a meaningful life emerges. This is the point of living the principles in the *Little Book*.

If you're reading this and feel that there are so many things in your life that you didn't create, please take a moment to catch yourself before you block out what is being given here.

> *Whatever is in your life is there for YOUR growth. Not someone else's growth. Your growth.*
>
> *Everything occurs for you to see what is needed WITHIN YOU. Whether you decide to be responsible for*

uncovering this truth is your choice to make. That's what is meant by responsibility.

How you respond to what happens to you will either link you more closely to your Soul or move you further from it.

The Energy of You

As you consider your situation, how you respond to life events, and what you might wish to improve, there is an important link to who you are—your energy. Most of us have not been taught one thing about our energy, except to define when we are tired or excited. That's a limited view of what is actually a vital part of your everyday life.

The fact is that humans, just like all matter, are made up of energetic waves that come together in a form. In our case, it's our body. Other forms would be trees, rocks, animals, radio signals, paper, cars—and the list goes on. Every scientist will confirm that all matter is moving energy, configured in a certain way. We give labels to everything and then perceive these things to be solid rather than energetic. The fact is that you, like everything around you, are vibrating at a certain energetic level.

This concept of you as an energetic being is important to grasp because it's a key part of being responsible for your life and it provides you with a way to create a fulfilling life. It's really your job to uncover your true energy essence. What is the *you* that exists without interference from everyone else? When you are quiet, calm, and focused within, how would you describe your energy?

If you cannot yet answer these questions or feel unclear about the concept, it's a good indication of where to start your journey. You must shift into a learning mode to uncover more knowledge about this part of yourself. Odds are your formal education didn't include one minute on teaching you about your energy. Yet it is so critical to your happiness.

Some simple ways to understand energy start with situations you experience. Have you ever walked into a restaurant, felt a bad "vibe," and decided not to eat there? Or met someone you've never known and felt like you've known that person all your life? Or had a conversation with someone in which what they say in no way matches what you feel from them? These are *energetic* experiences. You are picking up on the energy around you, instantly interpreting it and making a conclusion.

A wonderful illustration of how energy works is to picture a mother and daughter. In this case, imagine a negative relationship where the daughter always feels guilty when making decisions and ends up fighting with the mother, who of course, claims she's not doing anything at all. When you look at the energetics of their interaction, here's how it works: Both have a long history of this dance, so before they even meet, they are prepped for the drama. The daughter makes a decision to go away for the weekend, sending a defiant energy to the mother, claiming her right to do so. She casually states the facts, but the energy she sends is of independence and a "stand my ground" orientation. The mother anticipates this moment and begins sending her energy out into the room.

She literally sends it out, surrounding the daughter. Remember that the mother sees her daughter as an extension of herself, someone who needs her help in decision making. Yet the daughter wants no help at all. So one of them is holding her energy in, to herself, while the other is spreading it everywhere in an attempt to hold on. The impact is dramatic.

The daughter fights back, saying she can never do anything she wants. The mother states that she only wants the daughter to do what she wants to do and isn't interfering at all. Usually, the mother—known for guilting the daughter into changing her plans—will pretend that she doesn't care. Yet the daughter reads her energy and knows otherwise.

We are all doing the energy dance with each other. A business negotiation is another good example of how energy moves between people. Anger, frustration, and finally compromise. Many, many words are exchanged, but it's the energy that is shifting.

One of the easiest ways to witness how your energy affects another is with animals. When you are angry, reach out to touch your cat or dog and see what happens. Notice that they will run away or cower, even though you aren't saying anything. Then, drop into your heart, recall a loving experience, and then reach for them. Quite a different reaction.

Animals read energy, not words. Even with our rescue dogs, we are clued into their energy at all times and their reaction to people. When they bark or growl or snarl, we review the interaction to more clearly see what's triggering it. People often tell me that someone, even a good friend, enters their house and their dog just doesn't like the person. They can't understand it because this is such a good person. The bottom line is that the animals could not care less what the person says—they feel that person's energy. Their reaction is an honest reading of that person. One adopted dog we placed kept barking at the adopter's best friend. With an understanding of energy, they were able to discuss this and explore the reason why. Turns out that the friend was afraid of the dog and felt uncomfortable, but she had never said that out loud. The dog felt it, of course.

Dogs are more skilled at reading energy than we are. All animals are skilled at this, so why are we so uneducated? Why is this so foreign to understanding who we are? Because we just haven't been given any tools. Remember that we are gaining more knowledge all the time about the combination of mind, body, and spirit. We are still in our infancy in our level of expertise. This energetic component is new to most everyone. So do you want to learn more? Are you willing to admit you know almost nothing or very little? I hope so, because you're in good company, and this type of learning is so rewarding.

The Energy Dance

Try one day when you focus on sensing energy between yourself and others. Shift your attention from words to energy. Take time to reflect on each situation and what you felt, what they sent, what you sent. Just see if you can begin catching the energy dance. It's your responsibility to sharpen your awareness.

Practicing can be fascinating. Place yourself in a scenic setting where you feel most comfortable—in a meadow, the woods, the water, walking by trees, somewhere in nature. The energy and rhythm of nature will free you to release the energy that is not yours. Remember how you shift to a calmer, more "clean" feeling after being outside for a while? That's because nature has a cleansing affect on your energy. So start there. Really breathe, bring yourself into the present moment, and focus on your Soul. Give yourself time to let go of all the mental noise.

Once you can sense that your energy has shifted and the noise is gone, then you are ready to experiment. Enter a store and see what you sense. Call a friend and see how you experience the change in yourself. Read something that disturbs you and notice what happens. Watch a romantic movie and notice your energy.

This process of understanding the energy dance gives you such moment-by-moment practice that you can then begin to choose what you do in those moments.

The whole point of understanding energy is that you can then choose how you feel, moment by moment. You are responsible for your energy and your energetic interactions with others. And, most important, you stop compromising your own energy with regard to how you let others impact you.

Do you notice the difference between this versus feeling like a victim? You are in charge of your energy as well as what you let in. You become responsible for the energetics. Nothing happens to you. You understand the dynamics quite differently once you understand energy.

When I first learned about energy, I began noticing simple situations that clarified what I was being taught. If I had a rough day, angered by some event and then jumped into the car heading somewhere, I'd inevitably end up in a traffic jam. The outer event reflected my inner state, which if not conscious, meant I could release my anger and annoyance at the delays and have an entire dramatic episode. What a waste of energy. Now knowing what I know, if this situations occurs, I immediately trace back to the previous moments to uncover what triggered my change in energy. Then, once I know the state of my energy (remember, not my mind, but my energy), then I begin breathing and calming myself to release the energy more responsibly, rather than on others.

One city that provides some understanding of unconscious behavior is New York City. Many, many people are angry about things in their lives and rather than consciously work on handling those emotions, they dump them on others. Most visitors tell of encounters with angry taxi drivers or waiters or some other unprovoked incident, nonetheless directed at them. Of course, once you understand consciousness and responsibility, you know how unfair these harmful episodes really can be. If you've ever traveled in a taxi or walked the streets of Manhattan or another big city, it's a great way to test your own energetics, as well as experience exactly what I'm describing.

When you're first beginning to notice how energy works, you'll find your reactions are still automatic. Events and people will trigger you. Over time, with practice, you can actually manage your reactions. You no longer waste your energy or give your energy to others for their use, and you no longer use your energy in hurtful or exploitive ways.

Plus, if you want to create the life you want, you now have the energy you need to do so. Isn't that the point?

A male executive I coach told me that he now preps himself energetically prior to every meeting. Whereas before he'd go from one meeting to another, just plowing ahead, he realized the result wasn't what he wanted. Depending on his energetic state (regardless of what he or others said), he'd end up with confusion, delays, and unfocused interactions. Now he manages himself and the meetings very differently, all because he is responsible for this unseen and yet important part of himself.

Another great way to illustrate energy is the dynamic of a love relationship. Both partners supposedly love the other person so much that they only want what's best for him or her. The truth is that when any change threatens one or the other, the first thing that happens is that they fear losing their partner and will *energetically* send very mixed messages. Psychologists have long labeled the "enabler" in alcoholic families as the one who keeps the person drinking so he or she can maintain a role in the family that matters. Love relationships work in a similar way, where the words and energy often conflict. It's no wonder a couple finds themselves fighting or losing interest: The energy is shifting and they have no awareness of what is actually going on. One thing is being said and another is being experienced.

Answers Are Inside

As you begin to learn about your energy, refer to the other chapters in the *Little Book,* because each is related to helping you succeed with this new orientation. Responsibly handling your energy means tuning inside, using your intuitive skills, and breathing, quietly finding your inner rhythm. It also means staying in the present moment. If you flash ahead, your energy changes; if you return to a past moment, it also changes. Only in the present can you effectively manage your energy and then, in turn, respond appropriately to the energy of others.

And remember that your beliefs impact your energy. When you think of abundance, do you feel relieved or a bit fearful? When you focus on the potential of Divine Order, do you feel invigorated or afraid? Notice how beliefs shift your energy. These are things you begin to catch and change. Recurring energy themes signal where you can focus for changes.

A client always found herself agitated by her partner when she began handling money. She'd be paying the bills and shortly thereafter, end up in a fight over something else. In understanding energy, she could quickly retrace her steps to the fears she sensed about money, then realize that rather than releasing those, she carried them into another situation which then triggered an argument. Of course, the partner had no clue as to what had happened . . . it "came out of the blue". Being responsible for her energy, she could then explain it and they could both release the fight because both of them had greater awareness.

Another client was in the middle of a job change, working with me for months to shift his energy enough to allow a long-desired, new career course. He knew his fears would create some obstacles since he had wanted this new job for at least ten years, but had been afraid to go after it. What he failed to take into account was his family's reaction. Their energetic reaction to change impacted his ability to follow through with the decision. As the time grew near, his wife became worried and depressed with all the new changes that would occur and began to "throw" her fearful energy onto him. He had sleepless nights, felt agitated during the day, and found himself delaying return calls to his prospective new boss. He was beginning to sabotage his opportunity.

As we talked through this process, he realized that he was internalizing her energy and beginning to actually think it was a bad decision for him. At one point, the energetic impact was so great, he was ready to stay in the job he hated for another ten years in order to feel everything was "back to normal." I'm happy to say he waded through weeks of managing this energetic confusion and now has taken his new job. Though he couldn't directly tell his wife that she irresponsibly handled her energy, he was able to separate himself enough from her in order to do what was in his best interest, and ultimately in her best interest. He knew being enslaved in the wrong job was never going to make him a fulfilled person or a fulfilled partner.

Why This Matters

The bottom line in finding the link to your Soul is to take responsibility for how you are, what you need to heal, and what you need to learn. We all benefit as each of us gains greater awareness.

We stop anger from happening at inappropriate times, we stop controlling others wrongly, and we stop blaming others for our misfortune. We clean up our energy in relation to others, which then allows us to honestly connect to our Soul.

I have a favorite expression about energetic cleanup work. I ask clients to watch when people "throw up" on them. What I mean is that other people literally throw their energy out on you and it feels like you need a shower to get back to being yourself. We all know someone like this, yet we might not have recognized that it's the energy that we object to—not the person. But it's also important to check ourselves. When are we throwing up on someone? It's a graphic expression that perfectly illustrates what we do to each other all the time.

Energy is a fascinating area to explore. More is available to help you than is written here. This is meant to open a door that you may not have known existed. I assure you that if you responsibly commit to this area of personal growth, your life will change positively and quickly. Seek out teachers and resources to educate yourself. There is new learning available all the time.

CHECKPOINTS: *Where Are You Now?*

- Are you ready to throw out a lot of what you know and open up to new beliefs that reshape who you are?
- How open can you be to a new awareness?
- How willing are you to follow through on a commitment to your growth?
- Is your Soul enough of a priority now?

Principles for Reflection

Work with these principles:

- *What you have in your life you create. Nothing happens to you. You are not a victim. Instead, you are given opportunities to grow and wake up to a greater consciousness of what your life means.*

- *Once you entrust your life to a greater force of wisdom— your Soul—then disappointments become clear indicators of areas for growth. Growth as in work on yourself.*

- *This orientation of looking in the mirror is a responsible one, where you understand the dynamic principle— you create your life. Your life does not just happen to you. Your orientation creates what you experience.*

- *When you are connected to your Soul, you minimize a great deal of suffering because you finally are on course. Your life is aligned with the deepest part of you and what you came to do. The inside and the outside are in sync.*

- *The whole point of understanding energy is that you can then choose how you feel, moment by moment. You are responsible for your energy and your energetic interactions with others. And, most important, you stop compromising your own energy in how you let others impact you.*

- *The bottom line in finding the link to your Soul is to take responsibility for how you are, what you need to heal, and what you need to learn. We all benefit as each of us gains greater awareness.*

Continuing the Journey

Now that you've completed *The Little Book of Everyday Soul*, I hope you've gained a deeper insight into how to actually connect with your Soul. The journey is a step-by-step process, with twists and turns, clarity and confusion, failures and successes, but in the end the benefits outweigh the challenges.

There is a tremendous satisfaction that comes from living from your heart. The world around you is reshaped to match what resonates with your heart. The feelings of emptiness, confusion, and lack of belonging are diminished. These feelings are replaced by profound contentment, unparalleled joy, and a sense of purpose that will guide you through everyday decisions and activities.

The purpose of the Little Book is to help you make this transition from head to heart. Many, many things will compete for your attention in life, yet I hope that the answers given here provide you with a way to stay on course. This is *your* life, *your* purpose, and *your* right to bring forth the gifts that only you can give. Please seek out the inner connection with your Soul so that your life will be more meaningful and satisfying.

Your Soul is already guiding you. It always has been. Now, it's time to reconnect more consciously and bring the inner you to the outer world.

Lillie may be reached at sweetbcrescue@citlink.net or visit www .glenhighlandfarm.com to find out more about her sanctuary.

INDEX